ON GOLF

Timothy O'Grady is the author of *Curious Journey: An Oral History of Ireland's Unfinished Revolution* (with Kenneth Griffith), *Motherland*, which won the David Higham award and *I Could Read the Sky* (with photographs by Steve Pyke), which won the Encore award. His most recent novel is *Light*, published by Secker & Warburg in 2004.

ON GOLF

Timothy O'Grady

YELLOW JERSEY PRESS
LONDON

Published by Yellow Jersey Press 2004

2 4 6 8 10 9 7 5 3 1

First published in Great Britain in 2003 by
Yellow Jersey Press
Random House, 20 Vauxhall Bridge Road,
London SW1V 2SA

The Random House Group Limited Reg. No. 954009
www.randomhouse.co.uk

A CIP catalogue record for this book
is available from the British Library

ISBN 0–224–06113–5

Typeset by SX Composing DTP, Rayleigh, Essex
Printed and bound in Great Britain by
Bookmarque Ltd, Croydon, Surrey

For Edward J. O'Grady

We saw elderly citizens playing at the Old Scots game of golf, which is a kind of gigantic variety of billiards.

Peter Morris,
from *Peter's Letters to His Kinsfolk* (1819)

In this game you got eighteen holes
To shoot your best somehow.
Where have all my divots gone?
I'm in the back nine now.

Golf clubs are made of wood and iron,
They are not magic wands.
Balls drop in the sand trap.
Balls drop into ponds.
Balls drop into ponds . . .

I don't know about you, but I got to have me
    a few
When we get to that clubhouse bar.
It's my reward for this scorecard.
I'm way over par.
I'm way over par . . .

Loudon Wainwright III

I

The Shot

IT IS NEARLY IMPOSSIBLE TO HIT A PURE GOLF shot. Let us say that you are of similar dimensions and constitution to me. The ball, the smallest in sport save ping-pong balls and marbles, lies on some problematic surface of grass, weed or tarmacadam around six feet away from your eyes at the end of a long slender stick which you are clutching probably with a haunted uncertainty and turbulent viscera. The little ball weighs 1.62 ounces and is 5.28 inches in circumference. Let us say that the stick which you have in your hands is my nearly antique Wilson-manufactured Walter Hagen blade four iron, its face from hosel to toe measuring 2.7 inches along its base. In order to execute the shot the head of this four iron must be drawn away from the ball and travel some 270 degrees up and around your body and then return along a nearly identical path to make the strike, a distance of 47.12 feet. You will have begun this curiously ungainly action, which seems to have as many moving parts as an early piece of farm machinery, from a position of dead stillness, but by the time you strike the ball the clubhead will be travelling at just under a hundred miles per hour. In order to deliver a solid blow to the ball, the correct 0.049 square inches of the clubface must meet a theoretical point on the surface of the ball, a point which might realistically be described as comprising around a tenth of the area of the nail on your little finger. The ball will stay on the clubface for only .00045 seconds before beginning its unpredictable journey. If the correct part of the clubface meets the correct part of the ball you will make a solid impact, but this will not necessarily result in a successful shot, for the line of the clubface must be precisely perpendicular to the proposed line of flight to the flag, which rests around 180 yards away from where you are standing. An error of two degrees in alignment will result in the ball missing its target by around twenty feet to the right or left. Missing the centre of the clubface by a quarter of an inch will reduce the distance the ball travels by seven to nine per cent, or up to 48.6 feet. Each further degree of error will deposit your ball deeper into trouble, raise your score and compound your feelings of anguish and humiliation and abject worthlessness.

You are somewhere out on a golf course as you face this shot. You will have begun your journey of eighteen holes some five miles and four hours from where you will eventually complete it. Let us say that you are on a long par four measuring 440 yards and that you have hit a good drive of 260 yards to the centre of the fairway, leaving you with this 180-yard four iron. If the fairway is forty yards wide and the rough which can reasonably be said to belong to this hole is ten yards deep to either side and if we add on another ten yards behind the green, then the total area of the hole would be around 27,000 square yards. The little hole which is your destination has a diameter of 4.25 inches. In order to make the par which you now tremulously demand of yourself you must cause the ball to traverse this vast area and find its way into the little hole in four blows. As Arnold Haultain says in his fine little book *The Mystery of Golf,* 'A tennis-player has a whole court in which to play; a cricketer a whole field; the golfer has to put his ball into a hole of the size of a jam-pot, a quarter of a mile away.'

Depending upon where you are playing as you stand over this shot you might be facing, as I have at various times in my golfing life, sand, a pond or river, trees of tropical, Mediterranean or Nordic origin, heat, rain, snow, wind, a cliff face, ocean or mountainside, scrubland such as is normally only seen in cowboy films, a glacier, ankle-clutching vegetation, cactus, a lava bed, wild elk, alligators, ball-stealing monkeys, bears or the screamed blasphemies of bare-torsoed, pot-bellied, knobbly-kneed, beer-can-strewing citizens who should be required to submit themselves to the tutelage of an experienced Scots links player before they are again allowed onto a golf course. If your play on this day is variable and the match is intense you might pass through a range of emotion in the course of the round such as could otherwise take you a month to experience. You might even pass through such a range of emotion on this single shot.

To help you make your way around the golf course taking the least number of strokes you are allowed fourteen different clubs, each designed to advance the ball a specific distance or, in the case of the sand wedge and putter, out of or over a specific surface. You must know the distance you hit each of these clubs depending on the surface you are hitting off and the combination of climatic, emotional and physical conditions prevailing in or around your being at the time. These variables are compounded greatly in the case of the professional, who can hit each club in fine gradations of distance and high or low or with draw or fade according to what the shot requires. The variety of shots demanded of a golfer is more multitudinous than in any other ball-striking game. In fact no golfer will ever face precisely the same shot twice.

As you play your round you will look upon these clubs, as you will look upon your own body, as your enemies or your friends according to the state of your mind, for mind is all in golf. To hit this particular 180-yard four iron or any other golf shot all the technicalities of the swing must be internalized in the muscles, the thinking process must be shut down, and the mind must apprehend the ball with an intense purity and concentration. When a professional instructs a beginner to keep his eye on the ball he is doing so not for mechanical reasons or for the purpose of orientation, but rather to direct the student towards a simple, uncluttered yet hyper-aware state of mind. If obscure thoughts about the pronation of your wrists, where your hands are at the top of your backswing, or the rotation of your hips begin to rise into your mind like birds flushed from grass, or if you veer into the caves of doubt or fear or the sense of futility or even ridiculousness, then you must have at your disposal some mechanism that stops thought again and allows the mind simply to see. This is not easy. Temples and rented rooms all over the world are full of students of meditation striving for a similar effect. You can learn a great deal about how ugly and cacophonous can be the music of your mind by waiting for a moment of panic and disorientation on a golf course and then observing what is happening in your head. You are unlikely to have to wait long. It is like the sound of a short-wave radio as you move through the bands.

At the beginning of his very entertaining book *The Bogey Man*, the American writer George Plimpton constructs an elaborate and astonishing metaphor for this condition. He imagines his own body as he stands over a golf ball as a fourteen-storey-high structure full of chambers and passageways and measuring instruments populated by a throng of Japanese navy men – lazy and dissolute enlisted men in the limbs and joints and lower reaches, and excitable, rice-wine-drinking admirals gathered on the galleries behind the eyes. 'In their hands,' he writes, 'they hold ancient and useless voice tubes into which they yell the familiar orders: "Eye on the ball! Left arm stiff! Flex the knees! . . ."', these instructions drifting through the huge structure until they arrive in garbled form at the drunk and distracted men who in response reach up from their stupors and pull a few levers, sending the whole apparatus lurching and tipping until it finally strikes the ball, the admirals then clutching each other as they look out of their gallery windows and shout, 'A shank! A shank! My God, we've hit another shank!'

Weather, hazards, lack of technique or practice, poor coordination, erratic biorhythms, hangovers, an unruly mind and statistical improbability –

these are just a few of the obstacles to hitting a pure golf shot. It is no wonder that Ben Hogan, considered by many to be the finest striker of the ball in the history of golf, once said, 'This is a game of misses. The guy who misses the best is going to win.' In the whole of Tiger Woods' miraculous millennial season, during which he won three consecutive major championships, he believed he hit only one shot of which he could be justifiably proud. It took place on the fourteenth hole at St Andrews during the British Open, which he won by eight shots. He had around 260 yards to the pin, a tight lie in the rough and a left to right breeze. There were pot bunkers guarding the green. He had to hit a high draw against the direction of the breeze that would carry nearly the entire distance and then land softly. The shot was blind and he had to line it up against a television crane. He used a three wood, and it worked. There are, of course, very few people on this earth capable of realistically contemplating such a shot, let alone being able to hit it. For most golfers, hitting a four iron 180 yards to within ten feet of the hole would be one of the most significant and memorable events of the week in which it happened.

The shot is the irreducible unit of golf, and though touring professionals must think of the 270 or so of them they will strike in the course of a tournament, for most golfers the single shot is what they define and redefine themselves by. A shot stands alone in the memory. It is part of the longer story of the hole and round, but it is also an end unto itself. It can be a calamitous outrage or a magnificence that seems to resonate through the years like a fine work of art. Let us move back to the moments preceding the hypothetical 180-yard four iron which began this discussion. The day is fine – bright, warm, just the smallest of sea breezes to cool and caress you. Your play as usual has been inconsistent, but you have just had the pleasure of that fine 260-yard drive with a slight draw into the heart of the fairway. The hole, as do all holes, had asked of you a question on the tee and you had answered at least this part of it well. You allow yourself the thought that perhaps this drive marked the beginning of something, that your game is about to find its focus, you are now finally going to play to your potential. Then you silence this thought. One shot at a time, you think. You walk forward with your playing companions. The ball glistens in the sunlight. You pace off the distance from the 150-yard marker. You check the direction of the breeze, the position of the flag. You remember the roll of the green. You select a four iron and stand over the ball. Feet, hips, shoulders square to the line of flight. Weight evenly distributed. Right elbow close to the body. Smooth tempo. Years of reading, thinking and practising form the history of this shot. Though you have hit thousands of golf shots in your life, what your playing companions will see if they look at your face is a look of intensity and hope, as if this experience is unique, and much depends on it. You take the club back and then move into the ball. In this moment you experience a kind of breakdown as though your body has been miswired. All its parts seem engaged in distinct, unrelated activities. Your breathing is wrong. You are temporarily blind. You hear the club thud into the earth half a foot behind the ball. A divot the size of a toupee flies up. As your sight is restored you see the ball galumphing like a drunk along the fairway before coming to rest forty yards from where you are standing.

You may be able to accept this. You may think that if you were to hit the next shot well enough you could still manage a par. You may even laugh. But then again you may not. A violent and enraged self-loathing may enter you like a poison injected into your vein. The excruciating ugliness of the shot has insulted the father who taught you, the years you have played the game, the true abilities you believe you possess, and most particularly your splendid drive. You may feel like tearing your liver out.

This feeling will almost certainly pass quickly. After a hole or two, after a few middling strikes, you will still remember the shot, but the sting will have gone out of it. But then there are those rounds in which this is your fate shot after shot. Skulls, shanks, snap hooks, pop-ups, jerked putts – all the vocabulary of misery around the entire eighteen holes. Memory does not dispose of such occasions so efficiently. They can stay with you like a virus. You can be walking along the street feeling reasonably all right and the thought of an entirely hideous round of golf three weeks earlier will steal up on you and lay you low.

Then there are the glorious shots. A long drive will give you a feeling of power. If it is a long drive from an elevated tee against a dramatic, mountainous background you also get the exhilarating sensation of flight, as if the ball is a piece of yourself. There is the delicacy of touch you can demonstrate to yourself by holing a downhill, breaking ten-foot putt which you need in a match. Bending a low, punched four iron under and around the branches of trees and up to the green can temporarily convince you that you are an artist. But the most glorious of them all for me are long to middle irons that fly directly at a well-protected flag. The memory of these can stay alive for years. Every golfer has them. Golf is unusual among sports in this. A mediocre athlete cannot hit a tennis ball 140 miles per hour, go airborne from the free throw line and slam dunk a basketball or run 100 metres in less than 10 seconds, no matter how many times he may attempt it. But from 150 yards or less virtually any golfer is capable of hitting at some point a shot that feels sublime and looks as good as anything he sees professionals doing on television. Golf, of course, is not the only thing in life that offers rich, profound and important experiences, but the feeling derived from a fine golf shot is unique. For most of us, certainly, it is rare. But rarity alone is not what gives the feeling its definition.

A fine golf shot is succinct. It is simple. It is unambiguous, indisputable and pure. The mind seems to clear a space in the memory around such a shot, so that you remember the moments before as well as the shot itself – the assessment of what it requires, the selection of the club, the silence as you stand over the ball. You draw the club back and as you begin the downswing everything seems to be moving a little slower than is usual, the ball seems large and to be seen with a particular clarity, you are more aware of your body and the unexpectedly wonderful synchronization of feet, hips, shoulders, hands. You feel entirely balanced and in possession of what you are doing. Your hands move down, the shaft kicks forward and drives the clubhead down and into the back of the ball, the smell of earth rises up as the divot flies and you can see the ball from out of the corner of your eye leave the club, strong, true, explosive. You feel the unimprovable solidity of the shot in your hands, your chest and down near the base of your spine before it rises up the nerves into your brain. Your head lifts. Your hands are high, your muscles loose, your balance intact as you watch the ball flying wonderfully, beautifully straight at the flag. You know that the shot is all that it can be from you, if only the club is right. You may feel many things in this moment – delight, physical fulfilment, modesty or its opposite, for example. One of them, whether you care to display or even admit it, is also likely to be astonishment.

A golf shot happens in a moment and in the moment it can overwhelm all the anxieties and miseries in your life and seem to define the essence of the best part of what you are. Once you have made it it is your possession. At least some small part of you can thereafter be described by it. In *Rabbit, Run*, John Updike describes Harry Angstrom hitting the drive of his life and creating a wordless metaphor in the sky in answer to the Reverend Eccles' question about what is missing in his marriage: 'He looks at the ball, which sits high on the tee and already seems free of the ground. Very simply he brings the clubhead around his shoulder into it. The sound has a hollowness, a singleness he hasn't heard before. His arms force his head up and his ball is hung way out, lunarly pale against the beautiful black-blue of storm clouds, his grandfather's colour stretched dense across the north. It recedes along a line straight as a ruler-edge. Stricken; sphere, star, speck. It hesitates, and Rabbit thinks it will die, but he's fooled, for the ball makes its hesitation the ground of a final leap: with a kind of visible sob takes a last bite of space before vanishing in falling. "That's *it!*" he cries, and turning to Eccles with a grin of aggrandizement, repeats, "That's it."'

A single fine shot is the seduction that will lure you back to the course and repeated seductions will rapidly escalate into the monomania of obsession. Golf was, I think, my first obsession. It struck me around the age of twelve. In this sense I suppose it taught me what obsession is and resonated within all the other obsessions that have governed, enriched and distorted my life since then. There is a recklessness in obsession, and also at times an amorality, but above all there is a deep immersion in infinitesimal detail. Throughout my teenage years I practised and played golf, I earned my wages from it, I read and talked and dreamed about it and pondered it in a way and to a degree that I did no other thing – until I fell in love when I was eighteen with a girl named Ruth Farrell and the lure of golf receded from its eminence. To love was later added writing and still later children, and golf was thereafter in a more congested space within my being. Yet at no time was it any less than

13

fascinating to me. I can and always could converse about it for hours, even days, without a diminishing of the fascination.

To those not similarly stricken such talk is of course absurd and excruciating. Words such as 'sublime', 'majestic', 'genius' and 'heroic' applied to men wearing clothes more suited to schoolboys as they bat a little ball around over-groomed land seem to them pathetic and contemptible. 'You'd think it was something important,' they say. 'You'd think there were lives at stake.' And when you look at them blankly and return to your feverish description of the incredible shot Tiger Woods hit at the fifteenth hole at Augusta they run from the room with their fingers in their ears. I know one elegantly framed woman who approached the game but then could not bring herself to hit a shot. 'All that "bend over, grip the club, stick your bottom out,"' she said. 'I couldn't go on. It just seemed too ridiculous.' But as Arnold Haultain points out, 'Golf is like faith: it is the substance of things hoped for, the evidence of things not seen; and not until it is personally experienced does the unbelieving change from the imprecatory to the precatory attitude.'

Golf simply catches you and you are thereafter in some way betrothed. I know of nothing else outside of life's elementals of work, love, sex, family that is like it. It will find your addiction gene even more rapidly than vodka or roulette wheels. I sometimes think that those taking their first timorous swings on a practice ground should be warned that once the initial barrier is passed there is no way back. There is just something so simply wonderful about being in good company in the open air with the sun on your back, the birds singing and the aromas of nature floating around you as you hit golf shots that fly high over the land straight at their targets. For a hole or two as the ball rises out of the heart of the club shot after shot the game seems beautifully simple. It also seems, in some remote yet tantalizing way, conquerable. You think to yourself, Maybe I can get there. The game becomes a quest. Everything about it becomes fascinating. It is the illusion of mastery that drives the obsession.

My father had this obsession, as do I. One day, he told me, he played seventy-two holes on a nine-hole course and was so exhausted afterwards that he couldn't raise himself out of the bath. Perhaps he enjoyed his obsession more richly than have I, for at his best he was a better player than I am (so far), and I think he had a better character for it. We spoke about golf together from the time it first gripped me until the time of his death. Our last conversations were about golf. Golfers speak about fine courses, technique, the achievements of the great. But the most entertaining talk about golf is anecdotal.

My father had many stories about golf and I believe he was skilled at the telling of them. One of them was about a man named C. J. Bansbach, who had several times been club champion at the Butterfield Country Club in Chicago in the 1940s and '50s. I don't believe I ever met C. J. Bansbach, but I heard about him often and knew he had a thin moustache, wore plus fours and was a fine player. Prior to my birth my father had also been a member of the Butterfield Country Club and had competed against C. J. Bansbach many times. The story concerned the death of C. J.'s father. There was a wake held at a Chicago funeral home which my father attended. He approached the coffin where the body was laid out, said a prayer and then turned to C. J. in order to offer his condolences. C. J. thanked him gravely and asked my father if he would mind coming with him for a moment as he wished to have a private word. My father followed him through the mourners to a separate room. He didn't know what to expect, but he was prepared to help his friend in whatever way he could. C. J. closed the door, stood in the centre of the room and assumed his address position, an imaginary golf club in his hands. He then looked up at my father with the helpless expression of the addict and began, 'Do you think if I were to move my right hand a little bit under the shaft . . . ?'

II

Father and Son

MY FATHER WAS A FINE PLAYER, BUT HIS GAME suffered from the troubling of my birth.

He was, at the time, forty-five years old. At his best he had played off a three handicap and when I was born would have been no worse, I imagine, than a five, or perhaps a six. Butterfield, where he was then a member, was out on the west side of Chicago not far from where he was born and raised, but when he married he moved with my mother to an apartment on the north side, more than an hour's drive away from the course. Golf at his level requires considerable maintenance. He was playing Saturdays and Sundays and sometimes on Wednesday afternoons while my mother stayed at home with me. He thought this unfair to her, so he resigned his membership. 'I did it in the winter,' he told me later. 'It was less painful.'

For some time he was a golfing vagrant, playing occasionally at public courses, or at clubs when he was invited. At weekends he went to supermarkets, amusement parks or for walks in the forest with my mother and me, betraying no sign of a longing to be elsewhere. Sometimes he hit balls during the long summer evenings at a driving range. Finally he joined a club attached to a course in the grounds of a US Navy airbase not far from where we lived. The course was acceptable, but no more, and the golf played there somehow less serious, less fun and less important for him than it had been at Butterfield. His handicap drifted upwards to nine. Something irreplaceable had gone from his precision of striking, his competitive edge and his touch, and this had happened because of me.

He was the middle of three children of a man and woman who had emigrated from small farms in County Kerry in the south-west of Ireland and then met and married in Chicago. My grandfather worked twelve hours per day, seven days per week, as a streetcar conductor. He would, I imagine, have known little of golf beyond that it existed and was played by others in places somewhere outside his orbit. My father's introduction to golf came when he began caddying at Westward Ho!, a peculiar name that sounds like the title of a wagon train movie but in fact paid homage to England's first golf course. Caddies have traditionally been allowed to play at American clubs on Mondays, when the courses are closed to members, so I suppose that is how he first took up the game. I don't know the rate at which he advanced, but I know from a story told me by a friend of his that he was deep in the obsession in his mid-twenties.

This friend's family had a house on a lake in Wisconsin around one hundred miles from Chicago, and the two of them went there once for a weekend. They were to play a match on the Sunday, but the night before they went from drinking hole to drinking hole and then to an all-night dance before winding up at a roadside diner for breakfast. At one point my father left to visit the outside toilet. He was gone for a long time. Finally his friend went out onto the porch to look for him. He heard some low moaning, looked down and discovered my father entangled in the shrubs. Evidently the Prohibition moonshine they had been drinking had unbalanced him. He was in considerable pain. They discovered later that he had cracked a rib. His friend got him back to the house and into bed and then went to sleep himself. He was awakened some hours later by a swishing sound in the living room. When he went out he found my father swinging a golf club with one arm. 'What are you doing?' he said. 'We have a match,' said my father. 'But you can't play,' said his friend. 'You're injured.' 'I think I can manage if I just use one arm,' said my father, and resumed practising. According to his friend, they did go to a golf course and play a match, which he says my father won. I find this last detail not very credible, but I can appreciate the motivation for including it, for he told me the story just a month after my father died and he knew how susceptible I was to accounts of his rakishness and heroism.

I think it was an opportunity presented by an injury incurred during the Second World War that drove my father's handicap down to the serious number of three. He was a thirty-six-year-old dentist in love with but not yet married to my mother at the time of the Japanese attack on Pearl Harbor, but he immediately enlisted in the US Navy. He went through basic training and was then seconded to the Marines for their operations in the Pacific. During a landing at Guadalcanal he injured his back climbing down the side of a ship. He was put in a makeshift medical unit in a cave on the island and then sent to New Zealand for a laminectomy, an operation I also had at almost exactly the same age. When he was well enough he was shipped to San Francisco, where he passed the remainder of the war administering dental care on a Navy base in the mornings and playing golf in the afternoons for free on some of the best courses in the western United States. Most American courses were made available to military personnel throughout the duration of the war.

I can no more remember first becoming aware

of golf than first becoming aware of eating, for in spite of my father's efforts at temperance with respect to the sport, golf seemed lodged in our home like another family member that had been born unassisted and ectoplasmically out of him. The angels on his trophies looked down at us as we ate. Sometimes in the evenings when I did my homework I could hear the faint click of ball on club as he practised his putting on the strip of carpet that led from my bedroom to the room with the television at the back of the flat. It was in that room that I sat with him to watch *Shell's Wonderful World of Golf* or the final rounds of tournaments. The seasons took some of their definition from golf – there were his rain-spattered windbreaker hanging on a hook in the kitchen after an early spring round, the trips by boat to the golf course from that same house on the Wisconsin lake where his friend had awakened to find him practising a one-armed swing and where we came to spend our summer holidays, the ritual autumn polishing of his golf shoes and the cleaning with brush and nail file of his clubs before they were put away for the winter. They then sat in a closet from October to the following April, inanimate yet somehow on the verge of life, like dolls in a fairy story.

There is a photograph of me taken in a park when I was around two years old holding a golf club in a proprietorial manner. But I did not begin to play then. By some standards I began late, when I was eight. I was going one evening with my father and mother to have dinner somewhere and we stopped at a driving range on the way so that he could hit a bucket of balls. Evidently I interrupted him and asked if I could hit a few myself, and he agreed. He had done nothing that evening or at any previous time to bring the game to me because he thought it better that I find my own way to it. He was the same many years later with dentistry. He thought it could be a possible profession for me and, with the idea of introducing me to it, invited me to his office on a Friday night, the day of the week he stayed late to do his laboratory work. Afterwards we were to go to dinner. When I arrived he took me into the laboratory and showed me a bridge he was working on and began to explain how he would go about completing it. 'That's fine,' I said, 'I'll wait for you outside,' and then went into his waiting room to read. I had no idea of what was at stake for him in this moment. He finally told me about it, with some amusement, more than twenty years later.

My reaction to golf was the antithesis of my reaction to dentistry. I went to driving ranges with him and took up a position on the mat beside his with my own bucket of balls. I practised putting on the same strip of carpet where he practised. I broke the glass top of a table swinging a seven iron in the living room. I went along with him and my mother on holiday rounds and was allowed to hit a few shots from time to time. As a teacher he was simple, classical, knowledgeable. Square set-up, overlapping Vardon grip, turn on a central axis with the head still, smooth tempo. 'You can't overpower a golf shot,' he said. Once when I ran loudly down some stairs he told me I should move fluidly, with my knees. 'Heavy-weight boxers wouldn't be like that. They'd be silent. Strength is something graceful. Look at golf.'

Then there were those allegorical injunctions – 'Commit yourself to the shot', 'Don't give up on it', 'Smooth acceleration from the top of the back-swing', 'Keep your head down', 'Follow through'. You can see the reasons for such instructions by looking at poor players, particularly from a distance. Their swings are short and fast and nervous. They bring the club around their bodies from outside to in rather than extending their arms outwards on the follow-through and then slap at the ball with their weight on the back foot. This is due to a fear of losing a control they do not possess. They look up before completing their swings because of their anxiety to see where the ball is going. They set up with open stances for the same

23

reason. It is all nervousness, timidity, fear of failure. A good golf shot from a swing such as this is merely a matter of luck.

A good golf swing seen from a distance, on the other hand, looks smooth, slow, well balanced and controlled. This comes from hitting thousands upon thousands of shots. But in the fullness of the backswing and of the extension of the arms as they move into and through the ball, the head kept down and back as the body advances and turns, there must be an element of faith in oneself as the body enters the hitting area and then releases itself into the unknown. You need those things my father spoke about to get through this – a solid base, a movement beyond where your fears would like you to stop, then a kind of controlled abandon. But in retrospect, there seems more that can be taken from those admonishments than just tips for golf, spoken as they were by father to son.

Most of my golf for the first few years was played at a nine-hole course near the Wisconsin lake where we went for our holidays. I played with my mother and her women friends while my father played with the men. I played with my mother one summer afternoon in front of a man who hole after hole hit his tee shots before we were out of range. None had hit us but some had come quite close. We couldn't let him through because there were others ahead of us. My mother called out to him to be more careful, but the bombardment continued. Finally we reached the last hole. My mother and I had hit our drives into a hollow invisible from the tee and were waiting to hit our seconds when my father walked out to meet us. He asked us how we were doing. We said we were doing all right but that the man behind us had been hitting into us throughout the round. Just then a ball came over the hill and whistled past me two inches from my nose. My father took a three wood from my bag, walked over to the man's ball and hit it directly back at him. His woods and long irons had a wonderful shape to them that I have never been able to attain – starting low to the ground, then rising and drawing, rather like Arnold Palmer's. He hit this one beautifully, as shots struck in anger some-times are. I watched the ball sail over the hill and imagined it crashing into one of the upper branches of the high trees around the tee and then dropping onto the man's head just as he was returning his driver to his bag.

None of my neighbourhood friends played golf, until the Dore brothers took it up. The Dore brothers were good students and superb athletes and after conquering all around them in the conventional sports had set up a one-hole golf course at the school playground. This playground was a tarmacadamed rectangle containing three basketball nets and was bordered on two sides by streets, one side by the convent housing the nuns who taught us, and finally the last side by the backs of houses. The hole laid out by the Dores began with a tee set up in the grass adjacent to one of the streets, traversed the short part of the playground, narrowed to just a few feet as it passed through the gate to their house and ended in a hole which they had dug in their backyard. They knew of my interest in golf and invited me to play their hole. The shot now would be half a wedge for me, but we all used drivers. I hit a low line drive that passed through the gaps in the fence of their neighbours' house to the right, flipped a wedge from their lawn into the Dores' yard and then two-putted for a four. This, the Dores told me, was the course record, the only one I will surely ever hold and one that has not been broken, for the course was closed that afternoon due to complaints from neighbours.

My contemporaries moved collectively into golf when we reached the age when we could begin caddying. We caddied at the Edgewater Golf Club, a private club with wealthy members and tight fairways which was set down in an urban neighbourhood. If you hit a bad slice on any of the first five holes your ball could end up in a drive-in restaurant, a used-car lot or someone's bedroom. The club closed in the early 1970s and there is now a city park with a nine-hole course on the land, but Edgewater has a small place in the history of golf because it was the home course of the legendary Chick Evans, winner of three major championships in the early years of the twentieth century. Some would say that from tee to green he was the best of his time, but he remained an amateur. He simply couldn't picture himself as a pro, he explained. As a child he had caddied at Edgewater and he maintained a relationship with the club throughout his life. He was much sought after as a caddy because he found balls others couldn't by lying flat on the ground then rotating himself like a rolling pin through the rough. Years later, he set up a scholarship foundation which has sent hundreds of caddies to university. By the time I knew him he was an elderly, perpetually smiling man with a propensity for poetic flights of language. My father was his dentist and also played quite a lot of golf with him. I have a letter to my father from Chick praising his dental skills and his golf swing in a single lyrical and rapturous sentence.

I worked at Edgewater for six summers from when I was thirteen until I entered university and it formed the setting for a rite of passage for me perhaps like, in another era, running away with the circus. As I was to discover again later, and contrary to received beliefs, the world of golf has a highly varied populace, perhaps more highly varied than most other sub-sections of society. I met people at Edgewater I would almost certainly never otherwise have met. I met churchmen and pillars of the bourgeoisie. I met Mafiosi, scholars, bankrupts, teenage gang members, millionaires, Mexican guitar players, movie stars, professional gamblers, gigolos and other sexual adventurers.

There was an itinerant band of professional caddies allowed to work at the course in spring and autumn when schoolboy caddies were scarce. They were for the most part alcoholics, wanderers, men who could find no permanent place into which they could fit. They sat under the trees near the caddy shack and drank cheap sherry out of paper bags. They all seemed to have nicknames. I remember one in particular, a tall, haunted-looking man known as 'Al the Eye' because of a large empurpled deformity in that part of his face. If you paid them they'd buy you beer.

Up to that time my knowledge of sex was limited to what I could gather from very often misconceived playground badinage and one dour, dispiriting lecture with anatomical charts given us by one of the parish priests. At Edgewater I met it everywhere. I saw a friend of my mother's whose husband was away arriving at the club one evening with a bachelor member in his open-topped Cadillac. She was laughing, the wind was blowing through her hair. She had on a little dress with polka dots. When she saw me her eyes widened and she blushed. When she said hello to me she stammered. She later became very religious and I wondered if that moment had anything to do with it. I heard a rumour, elaborated by locker-room attendants, that a member tried drunkenly to mount an inflatable doll with simulated parts in a small sleeping room. He'd left the door ajar, apparently. Every morning I had breakfast with a lesbian named Jamie, the locker-room cook. She lifted weights, rolled her packets of Lucky Strike cigarettes in the sleeve of her T-shirt and lived in a trailer behind the fourteenth green with a long-legged, languorous, spectacularly beautiful red-haired waitress whose shape could give you vertigo. One of the Mexican greenskeepers made a pass one evening at the waitress and Jamie hit him so hard that he went rolling backwards down the kitchen stairs all the way to the cellar. One sunny morning a fellow caddy sat in the grass by a tee as we waited for our group to hit their drives and told me about the powerful effect you could produce in girls by licking between their toes. 'That's what they like more than anything,' he told me. For the members we were very often invisible, so we heard many details of their lives, financial, domestic, sexual. I remember Jim Flanagan, a tall, long-hitting southerner with a two handicap, fitting on a new golf glove, running his fingers over the leather palm and saying, 'As smooth as the inside of a schoolteacher's thigh.' That seemed then, as it does now, astonishingly precise and privileged information.

The actor Martin Sheen once worked as a caddy and said that the experience taught him at an early age how ugly is the exercise of privilege. Caddies are like barmen in their quick acquisition of a jaded sense of humour due to repeated close observation of the foibles and grotesqueries of the rich and powerful while remaining unobserved themselves. There is a joke about a spoiled and boorish American playing in Scotland who blasphemes and throws clubs as he tops, shanks and slices his way around the course before finally turning to his caddy after a missed putt and exploding, 'You are absolutely the worst caddy this game has ever seen!' The caddy takes a draw on his cigarette. 'Oh no, sir,' he says. 'That would be too much of a coincidence.'

At Edgewater we sat around the caddy shack trying to outdo each other in our imitations of the idiocy of the members. The only ones excluded from this were a group known to us as 'The Boys', seven or eight low handicappers who played every day at around eleven o'clock for very high stakes.

We were in awe of them. We were in awe of them because they played for such large amounts of money, they were good golfers and they tipped better than anyone else. They played a game with six possible points available on each hole, starting at $20 a point, with repeated pressings, or doublings, until the stakes reached $320 per point or more. There were also side bets. These men had businesses that evidently needed little scrutiny from them. One sold perfume, another provided security guards. Jim Flanagan published a racing sheet. But there was one, Jack McGrath, whose only apparent income was from gambling at golf and cards at the club. He had a wife and at least one child, membership fees and living expenses to deal with, and played off a five handicap which he couldn't inflate because he played every day with the same people. He fascinated me. I couldn't imagine how he could do it.

One of the members on the periphery of this group was a thirteen handicapper named Mickey Mason who once went out and played another member for $1,000 per hole. He was bald and smoked fat cigars and boasted that he was the only Jew to evade the scrutiny of this racially exclusionary club. He had a regular caddy named Moose O'Brien who was immense and terrifying and used surreptitiously to roll the ball in the rough to improve the lie, though with or without his employer's knowledge I cannot say. Moose told us about going to a hooker and paying I believe $20 for an initial session and then $10 each for two more 'positions'. I tried for a long time to imagine what he meant by this.

Long after the club had closed and the members had dispersed and I had gone to live on another continent, I heard a story about Mickey Mason from a former Edgewater member who was a friend of my father's. Mason borrowed money from a gangster and when he couldn't make the payment at the appointed time the gangster organized the kidnapping of Mason's only child. The money was found and the boy was released. Mason then went to a golf course where he knew the gangster was playing. He found him out on the back nine somewhere waiting for his turn to putt. He walked up onto the green, pointed a gun at the man and said, 'That's the last time you fuck with my family.' Then he shot him dead.

I saw Bob Hope play at Edgewater and one of the men out of Peter, Paul and Mary, but far more impressive to me was Marty Stanovitch, the legendary hustler known in that beyond-the-frontier world of gamblers as the 'Fat Man'. He played cards, and I believe shot a little pool, but most of his income came from golf. He played big money games all around the country with players who knew all about him, including, I was to learn later, Arnold Palmer, but mostly he worked the resorts, applying pancake make-up in the mornings to disguise his tan and pass himself off as a newly arrived tourist. He might work on one person for more than a week, losing a couple of times and perhaps winning narrowly before moving in for the pay-off. Once he had his fingers broken on the West Coast.

He came to Edgewater when I was around sixteen to play a money match with 'The Boys'. I went out to the first tee to look at him. He was a short round man with sparse strands of greased-back hair and a pencil moustache. In my memory he looks a little like the corrupt grandee in Orson Welles' *Touch of Evil*. He kept his swing short and flat to get it around his high, tight stomach, and also, perhaps, to make it look unthreatening. He had a worn canvas bag stained with what looked like car grease. Both woods and irons were old, battered and mismatched. One of the irons had perforations in the face instead of grooves and an antique steel shaft painted a streaked brown to make it look like hickory. The whipping was coming loose around the neck of his driver. His clubs looked just as they were meant to look – like they had been bought at a jumble sale. Had I not known who he was I'd have felt confident of beating him.

A few hours later I watched him come up the

eighteenth hole. It was a par four which doglegged left and he had hit his drive beyond a line of trees to the right. There were about 160 yards remaining to the green and he had not only to hit the shot with a very steep trajectory but also to draw it around the trees, just clear a bunker tight to the right-hand front of the green and stop the ball quickly. The ball seemed to drop like a feather, twelve feet from the hole.

When I saw him in the clubhouse I asked him how he had played.

'I did lousy,' he said, spreading his hands. 'Sixty-nine.'

Many years later in a Park Lane hotel I heard a story about Marty Stanovitch from Barbara Romack, one of the leading American women professionals of the 1960s. She was on a brief European tour with a friend of my mother's. She asked me where the best casinos were and displayed an animated interest in gambling, something that is perhaps not uncommon among high-level athletes. I asked her if she knew Marty Stanovitch. She did, she said. During the off-season she toured with him sometimes, looking for money matches in the south and west. She told me that one day they were playing a match in California and as they were walking up the eighteenth fairway a young black man ran out from the clubhouse to meet them.

'Can we play tomorrow, Mr Stanovitch?' he asked.

'Sure.'

'Same time, same bet?'

'That's fine. I'll see you on the first tee at nine o'clock.'

The young man ran back to where he had come from.

'Who's he?' asked Barbara.

'He's a guy I've been playing with out here the last couple of years. He's got a lot of talent. But he'll never beat me.'

'Why's that?'

'He's strong, he hits the ball real good. But always with a draw. Even a nine iron he draws. So what I do is, I get up early and give the greens-keeper fifty bucks to cut all the pins front right. The poor guy can never get the ball near the hole. He just can't figure out what goes wrong.'

When later I was writing something about professional gamblers I wanted to include these men who ranged the open road with their golf bags in the boots of their cars, improvising, using their imaginations, looking for that finely calibrated edge, entertaining themselves and others as they preyed on human greed with their feats of leverage and deception. I called Barbara Romack in Florida to ask her where they were. 'They're gone,' she said. 'Extinct.'

I hung on as a caddy while a number of my friends went on to summer jobs as camp counsellors or construction workers or waiters. Eventually I became the regular caddy of one of 'The Boys', Bob Kane, a wild and very long eight handicapper with the strongest grip I'd ever seen, the Vs formed by thumb and forefinger improbably pointing to somewhere below his right elbow. I liked him very much, and I got to see at close range good players in tense matches for high stakes, but when I was offered a full-time summer job cleaning clubs and putting on new grips in the bag room I took it. The following summer I became assistant to the starter, a small diabetic former Scots professional named Charlie Pairman. These jobs provided me with my first regular paychecks. They also gave me access to the course. I could play all day on Mondays and each evening after the last of the members had gone out. The evening I came to see as my time, the day's work finished, family and other involvements of the night not yet begun, when I would go out alone with the air cooling and the sun low and the sound of birdsong and the whack of club on ball echoing in the tree-lined fairways. A golf course still looks at its most inviting to me at this time of day.

Golf had by my mid-teenage years assumed an imperial presence in my life. I read instruction books and golf magazines. I kept my sand wedge under the desk in the starter's office and whenever I could I hit shots from the bunker beside the ninth green. During afternoons in the school year when the weather was good I hit hundreds of nine-iron shots on a football field near our home. I had a yearning to see the thrilling high arcing shape of golf shots everywhere – out of classroom windows, along highways, from the tops of buildings. One afternoon I was waiting for a train after a round at a lakeside public course called Waveland. The Chicago Cubs baseball park, Wrigley Field, was adjacent to the station. There was no one around. I took out a four wood, teed up a ball between the wooden slats of the platform and hit it cleanly over the hoardings and apartment building rooftops and into the baseball park. At night in my bed in those years I played heroic rounds in my mind before going to sleep. I talked about golf incessantly. It felt sometimes like something I could not quite contain, like something from which I needed some relief.

On the larger stage of golf at that time two of the greatest players in the history of the game, Jack Nicklaus and Arnold Palmer, were battling for supremacy. The presence of Palmer in particular gave another dimension to many people's personal obsessions with the game – certainly to mine. Whether he won or lost, and how he did it, had an urgency and importance that I did not feel again until I watched Muhammad Ali fight Joe Frazier and George Foreman in the following decade. He seemed so different from the others, with their careful calculations, their masks of imperturbability, their smaller anxieties. He charged putts at the hole from 50 feet and beyond and crashed his driver off the fairway to water-encircled greens 280 yards away. His swing was a wild, ungainly, muscular explosion that almost no one could understand. Gary Player said that when he first saw him hitting balls sparks seemed to fly up from the grass. You could see everything that was happening inside him in his face, the anguish and the glories. It was like violently changing weather patterns. He played golf of the possible, however remote, rather than the probable. He was often to be found deep in a wood, grass and twigs flying up around him, his club waving before him and his torso bobbing like a middleweight's as he strained to follow the flight of his ball through a tiny aperture in the branches of a tree up ahead. Everyone watching him seemed as anxious and expectant as he did. 'Arnold would never protect a lead,' said Lee Trevino. 'He just kept firing for birdies. He'd go for the flag off an alligator's back.' At Augusta in 1964 he arrived at the par-five fifteenth on the final day with a lead over the field of five shots. After his drive he faced a long second shot to a shallow green protected by water at the front. Probably every other player in the tournament would have hit an iron safely short of the water were they in his position. He took his three wood and swung at the ball with tremendous force. As it sailed towards the green he lost sight of it in the late afternoon sun. 'Did it get over?' he asked his playing partner, Dave Marr. 'Arnold,' drawled Marr, 'your *divot* got over.'

I was too young to appreciate him during his best years, that stretch of 1958–64 when he won his seven major titles. By the time the mania truly had me in its thrall Nicklaus had more or less won the battle. But Palmer remained a threatening and compelling figure. He generated an energy in the game generally that people hacking away on courses all over the world could feel the effect of. As reading great literature can make you want to write, so watching Arnold Palmer made you want to play golf.

Those regular summer evening few holes I played at Edgewater provided me with a middling ability. When I was seventeen and eighteen I was playing off nine, or perhaps ten, while harbouring the illusion that my true game, the game that was inside me, was in fact much better than that. If only I had time to practise more, if only I got some good breaks, if only I could sort out the ridiculous and tedious business of chipping and putting, then, surely, I would play to my true potential. This is an illusion I have not ceased to chase, though at least I no longer believe chipping and putting to be ridiculous. I was on, then off, and then finally again on my high school golf team. In the Chicago Catholic League finals I shot eighty-two after hitting fourteen greens in regulation. The round included forty-two putts. Had I taken two putts per hole – which is not too much to ask, I told myself – I would have shot a four-over-par seventy-six and been one behind the medallist. Also, our team would have won the championship. My score that day seemed to be more an irrationality or bad luck or plague than flawed playing. Putting was something I thought extraneous to good golf. In some adolescent way I may even have been proud that my sound tee-to-green play had been undone by this fiddly activity at which even elderly ladies can excel. It certainly did not occur to me that I should learn more about this part of the game, and practise it.

I have never again played as much golf as I did in those years, but I only rarely played with my father. He had his playing companions and I had mine. We talked quite a lot about golf, however, and I was always interested in learning about his rounds. I remember the pleasure I had listening to his story about being drawn against a notorious cheat in his club's Class A Championship.

Whenever he tried to fix a time to play the match the other man declared himself busy. Finally the man suggested that they play separately and match scorecards later. For years my father had watched him collect trophies that were not rightly his. 'If I have to play you at midnight with a flashlight I will do it,' said my father. On the day that they played the match my father hooked his drive on the second hole and the ball came to rest against the trunk of a tree. He played it back out into the fairway left-handed using the reverse side of his putter. 'I'm afraid that's a two-stroke penalty as turning the putter around makes an extra club in your bag and that puts you over the limit,' said his opponent. 'But I'll overlook it this time.' This is incorrect, of course, as my father knew, but to be called a rule-breaker by a cheat and then magisterially absolved was more than was tolerable to him. He bore down and won the match six and five. 'It's best to play with a controlled mad,' said Sam Snead.

But about matters other than golf I was beginning to test the relationship, to goad him and push him towards and perhaps beyond his limits. At dinner I would summon whatever vituperative language I then had and in long monologues assault the hypocrisy of the Church, the immorality of American policy in Vietnam, the corruption of the bourgeoisie. He never quite took the bait. At times he agreed, at other times he held his ground. But he never lost his temper, though he must surely occasionally have found it wearisome. This is adolescence, this is, I suppose, the Oedipus complex, that psychological pre-disposition which Freud thought the most deeply embedded of all. The son craves the admiration of the father, but he also strives to surpass him, and in some figurative way to kill him.

We were fortunate, I think, to have golf to absorb some of this, to provide an arena in which the drama could play or at least talk some part of itself out. Most fathers and sons did not have this, for most did not share an activity in which they could compete as equals. Just after I graduated from high school and a few weeks before I fell in love with Ruth Farrell my father offered me a round of golf as a graduation present. I think it was the first round we would play together during that summer in which golf was to recede from its place of importance in my life. I was playing well, for me. I wanted him to see what I could do – particularly at the venue he had chosen, for it was heavy with symbolism. We were to play all twenty-seven holes at the Butterfield Country Club, the course on which he had probably played his most enjoyable and best golf and towards which he had felt compelled to turn his back upon my arrival in his life.

It was a still, sunny June day. We had lockers assigned to us and had lunch in the men's locker room. Various members and employees came over to greet him. I saw his name engraved on plaques as the winner of various competitions. We went out to the first tee. We were to play a warm-up nine and then proceed to the official eighteen. As at all private clubs, we were compelled to take a caddy, a great embarrassment to me as I had so recently been a caddy myself. I walked next to him and talked to him throughout the round in case I might be taken as the visitor's equivalent of a member's son, that human sub-species about whom the Edgewater caddies had been at their most corrosive. I don't remember much about the round, except a few singular sunlit images and the fact that I played solidly and avoided falling apart at any point. I had a thirty-nine on, I think, the second nine we played and an eighty or eighty-one over the eighteen. This was two shots or so better than my father. I also had the better score over the entire twenty-seven holes. I had beaten him. This had never happened before.

After I added up the scorecard I turned to him and said, 'I won.'

'It's about time,' he said.

Indeed it was. He was sixty-three and I was eighteen. Yet this made it no easier for him entirely to accept.

Not long after that round at Butterfield it all faded away, for then came Ruth Farrell, protest marches, cross-country hitchhiking, visionary literature, wine, music and rhapsodic talk through the night, and golf for a time became a small, nearly forgotten thing in my life.

III

Can Golf Save the World?

NO CIVILIZATION HAD AS PROFOUND A BELIEF IN the importance of sport as the ancient Greeks, but they did not invent golf. The Pharaoh Tuthmosis III hit leather spheres stuffed with wool and clay into the desert with a club carved from olive wood and the Romans played a game called *paganica* in which a feather-stuffed ball was batted down a street towards the opposition's goal, but neither of these activities could be described as golf. The invention of golf was evidently begun around 1300 in Holland as a game played with sticks and balls on frozen canals, the aim of which was to hit a stake embedded in the ice, and completed around one hundred and fifty years later by Scotsmen who added the defining presence of the hole. These holes were originally rabbit scrapes dug in sandy land near the sea and marked by gulls' feathers. No one knows for certain how it moved from Holland to Scotland. Some say it was Scottish wool merchants delayed by poor weather and introduced to what the Dutch called *kolf* by hospitable clients. Nor is it known why it was transformed into a game with a hole. But by 1457 there was already enough of a mania around it for the Scottish parliament to declare that 'the Fute-ball and Golfe be utterly cryit doune, and nocht usit'. It seems that these two games were interfering with soldiers practising their archery. There has long been a connection between golf and the military, from those earliest days to the founding in 1829 of the first golf club outside Scotland, the Dum Dum in Calcutta, by a Scots regiment stationed there, to the continued influential presence in golf of military men, particularly those austere and fastidious ex-officers who when retired go in for freelance proofreading and club secretaryships. It was soldiers with time on their hands who built the first courses in continental Europe and in Africa. Alan Shepard took golf to the moon.

There is a record of Musselburgh fishwives playing in competition in 1810, which indicates an early democratizing presence in the game. But golf was expensive. Balls imported from Holland cost so much that the Stuart court established an official ballmaker to undercut them. The balls in use for golf's first four hundred years were called featheries and it took one man an entire day to make two of them, each fashioned from two top hats full of boiled goose feathers and a leather pouch. Monarchs played it, particularly Scots. James I was a fanatic who overrode the Church's objections to golf being played on Sundays. Mary, Queen of Scots is said to have played golf days after Darnley's murder as a public display of her indifference. Charles I was on a course at Leith when he first learned of an insurrection in Ireland. James II played a big money match against two English noblemen with a poor shoemaker named John Patersone as his partner and Patersone won enough that day to build a new house.

Why Scotland? Is a nation expressed in its games? I don't know that country well enough to say, but Arnold Haultain advances a theory. 'Golf,' he says, 'is self-reliant, silent, sturdy. It leans less on its fellows. It loves best to overcome obstacles alone . . . There is something Puritanically and Sinaitically threatening in the thought of "approaching" a hole; as if, puir aperture, it were not to be come at but after due preparation thereunto, and were altogether fenced off from the ignorant, the scandalous, and the profane.' I suppose there is a severity to those grey Scottish skies and that even greyer Edinburgh stone, to the unadorned Calvinist churches and the messages handed down from their pulpits, just as there is a severity to golf. There is no absolution in golf as there is in almost all other sports, where you are constantly being presented with another chance.

In golf you can blow a four-day strokeplay tournament with a single errant shot. And in golf you stand alone, and exposed. There is no team in which to hide. But I think golf as a precise cultural or religious metaphor is an unsustainable idea. There are too many Catholics, for example, playing it well. Tiger Woods is in part a Thai Buddhist.

Having been moribund since the ancient Greek Games, organized sport exploded suddenly and spectacularly in Western society in the mid-nineteenth century, particularly in Britain. As the Caribbean writer C. L. R. James says in his great book about cricket, *Beyond a Boundary*, 'Golf was known to be ancient, but the first tournament of the Open Championship was held only in 1860.' He then points out that the Football Association was founded in 1863, the first modern athletics championship was held in England in 1866, the first English cricket team left for Australia in 1862, and the first professional baseball team was put together in the United States in 1869. This was of course a time of mass industrialization, of the mechanization of agriculture, and of the great expansion of cities, with their need for organized diversion and exercise. But James sees in it something more. 'Disraeli's Reform Bill, introducing popular democracy in England, was passed in 1865. In the same year the slave states were defeated in the American Civil War, to be followed immediately by the first modern organization of American labour. In 1864 Karl Marx and Frederick Engels founded the first Communist International and within a few years Europe for the first time since the Crusades saw an international organization comprising millions of people. In 1871 in France Napoleon III was overthrown and the Paris Commune was established . . . So that this same public that wanted sports and games so eagerly wanted popular democracy too. Perhaps they were not the same people in each case. Even so, both groups were stirred at the same time.' Intellectuals from Matthew Arnold to Trotsky dismissed sport as a trifle or a distraction. They could not see it as a form of self-expression, nor understand people's need to bear witness to it. They could not see it as Solon did when he answered a barbarian's question about the Greeks' obsession with sport by saying, 'I cannot find words to give you an idea of the pleasure that you would have if you were seated in the middle of the anxious spectators, watching the courage of the athletes, the beauty of their bodies, their splendid poses, their extraordinary suppleness, their tireless energy, their audacity, their sense of competition . . . their unceasing efforts to win a victory. I am sure you would not cease to overwhelm them with praise, to shout again and again, to applaud.' Forty thousand people used to gather in Athens for the original Olympics. Plato and Pythagoras always sat in the front row. Even Diogenes, the founder of Cynicism who dressed in rags and carried a candle as he looked for an honest man, came to the Games.

In addition to these social and political considerations, there was a technological factor in the opening-out of golf to the masses – the introduction of the gutta-percha ball in 1848. Gutta percha is a gum-like substance emitted from tropical trees which acts like a thermoplastic – it can be moulded when hot and hardens when cool. There is a legend that the Reverend Doctor R. Patterson invented the gutta-percha golf ball after receiving a statue of the Hindu god Vishnu from his half-brother, a missionary in India. The statue was packed in gutta-percha chips, some of which fell into the fire as the package was opened and melted in the heat. Reverend Patterson rolled one into a ball, which hardened when it cooled. He was struck by its resemblance to a golf ball and decided to take it out on the course to try it. He found that after the ball acquired the nicks and scratches it needed to get airborne it flew beautifully, considerably further than a featherie. It would also be more durable and far cheaper to produce: it could be mass-produced in a factory rather than handmade in a pro shop. The legend is almost certainly false, but what is known definitely is that while the gutta-percha ball was resisted by most professionals as both untraditional and threatening to their livelihoods, it was enthused over by Old Tom Morris, then an assistant pro at St Andrews but eventually as dominant a figure in golf as was W. G. Grace in cricket.

Intrepid, entrepreneurial and games-loving Scots, along with a few Englishmen, took the game out into the world. Courses were built in South Africa, Canada and Australia, usually commissioned by a Scots army officer or millionaire and then staffed by Scots teaching professionals and clubmakers. Golf grew steadily in these English-speaking imperial outposts. It took some time to settle in the United States. Three Dutchmen were fined in Albany, New York in 1657 for playing their version of the game on ice on a Sunday. 'Veritable Caledonian balls' were offered for sale in New York City in 1799, and there were perhaps courses of some description in Savannah, Georgia and Charleston, South Carolina as early as 1788 and 1811 respectively, but they faded away, as did another attempt to establish a club near White Sulphur Springs, West Virginia in 1884. Golf was finally established in the United States by John Reid, a Scot from Dunfermline who grew rich operating an ironworks in Yonkers,

New York. He had never played golf but he had an enthusiasm for games and asked a friend named Robert Lockhart who was visiting Scotland to bring him back some supplies. Lockhart bought a set of clubs and two dozen gutta-percha balls at Old Tom Morris's pro shop and Reid later tried them out on an improvised three-hole course in a cow pasture on a prematurely warm day in February 1888. Later that year, Reid, Lockhart and a few friends who came collectively to be known as 'The Apple Tree Gang' convened and founded the first lasting golf club in the United States, which they named St Andrews.

Since then, golf has exploded sensationally. It has for some time been the world's fastest growing sport. It can be played in all seriousness by infants and geriatrics and every age between. The one-armed, the blind and the wheelchair-bound play golf. Hackers and scratch players can compete on equal terms through the handicap system. Mass-manufacture and the proliferation of cheap public courses run by municipalities have brought the game within the reach of virtually anyone with a job. Many young men who might otherwise have thought that their experience of sport had ended with school are now taking up golf in exponentially increasing numbers. Golf is an enormous, ever-expanding business, important in real estate development, the media, corporate self-promotion and tourism. Golf courses are being built all around the world and there are now university degree courses in greenskeeping. Club and ball manufacturers are divisions of international conglomerates, at one end of which are the appetites of the shareholders and at the other those of the consumers.

In between is the industry itself. Central to it are the engineers who apply evolving ideas in aerodynamics to balls and test new metals and thermoplastics, lighter and with higher ballistic capacities, for clubs. Many of these substances have been developed by the defence and aerospace industries and have arrived at the club-manufacturing plants through scientific journals and university physics and engineering departments. Prototypes are cast, the workers on the factory floor guide them through the multitudinous stages of the manufacturing process, robots and professionals test them, ads are placed, brochures written in a promotional language of breakthrough, discovery and the promise of invincibility are distributed, and marketing men and reps go out by car and plane to try to sell them, the whole system struggling to prey on the illusion that golf is conquerable. Leading professionals are paid $1 million or more per year to have the names of these manufacturers stitched onto the sides of their bags.

Golf was once confined almost exclusively to the English-speaking world. It is now global. The golf industry traverses the world in search of new markets. Japan, Sweden and Argentina have been cultivated for decades, but much of the rest of the world is there to be worked. In South-East Asia and the Pacific, China, Russia and Eastern Europe there are new bourgeoisies being created who might be persuaded to see golf as a mark of status. These countries will also, of course, have their own genuine addicts.

Professional golf experienced two great leaps forward in the money made available to it and the status accorded it – first, in the 1920s, because of Walter Hagen, and then in the 1960s because of Arnold Palmer. These men had great victories, great charisma, great fame, great marketability. Professional golf has now entered a new epoch with Tiger Woods. He is perhaps the most globally famous athlete since Muhammad Ali. Television ratings leap whenever he is in contention in a tournament. Prize money has reached levels only recently unimaginable. Professional golf as a spectator sport now sustains a superstructure comprising the main US and European tours, various satellite tours for those who have not qualified for the main tours, special team and individual events, shorter winter tours in Africa and the Far East, numerous national and regional circuits, skins games, pro-ams, clinics and exhibitions.

But golf seems unlikely as a spectator sport. Almost all sports, apart from certain types of motor racing and cross-country skiing and running events, are played in a single arena in which all the action is simultaneously visible. Golf, of course, is not. If you go to a golf course to watch a major event you can follow a single group from start to finish, you can sit in a grandstand next to a green and watch the players putt as they pass through, you can run around trying to get glimpses of different players and different holes, or, perhaps most rewardingly of all, you can watch them hit balls on the practice ground. But you will never get the entire narrative of the day. If you try to see Tiger Woods you will have to do so over or around a great many other heads. If you don't have a stool or a periscope you may only see the sunlight flashing on the shaft of his club at the top of his backswing or follow-through. It is a highly fragmentary experience. On television you can at least get a sense of the entire picture of the event as it develops, but you will nevertheless spend most of your time watching the players trudge silently up the fairways or stalk the greens as they line up their putts or else following the progress of the white specks of their balls against the sky as the cameras waveringly track them.

There is no sustained action in golf. It takes only around two seconds to hit a shot, then the player spends up to ten minutes or more walking after it and waiting to hit the next one.

Yet people watch in great numbers. Some of the greatest fortunes in all of sport have been amassed due to the yearning of people to watch professional golfers. There are entire television channels devoted exclusively to it. There is even one in Spain, where golf is of only marginal interest.

What will be the effects of the great expansion of golf? Can golf transform character? Can it, when played by so many people of so many different ages and types in so many different places, change in some way the global social fabric? Has there been a social effect in England from the playing in schools, in military barracks and on village greens of cricket, that game so cunning and polite and vicious, or in America of the mass playing from so early an age of violent and fiercely competitive sports in which cheating is rewarded? I don't know. It would seem impossible to measure.

But if I were to speculate? There are, I would say, verifiably negative effects on society from the playing of golf. Of all games it is probably the most domestically intrusive. It takes nearly all day to play and get back and forth from the course, and then golfers talk about it during so much of the time when they are not playing. And there is no prospect of the intrusion on family life having an endpoint, for unless gravely handicapped or ill the golfer can play the game until he dies. There is a *New Yorker* cartoon depicting a man with a golf bag on his shoulder looking back at his wife as he leaves the house, saying, 'Gotta run, sweetheart. By the way, that was one fabulous job you did raising the children.'

Golf can generate terrible moods. Players so often begin a round in hope and end it in self-loathing. People who are normally equable and considerate can become surly, irritable and self-pitying. They can lose their sense of proportion about the importance in the larger scheme of things of their weight shift or the position of their elbows at the mid-point of their backswing. It can perhaps even permanently cloud a sensibility, or so Scott Fitzgerald seems to have thought when he wrote in *The Great Gatsby*, 'The bored haughty face that she turned to the world concealed something – most affectations conceal something eventually, even though they don't in the beginning – and one day I found out what it was . . . At her first big golf tournament there was a row that nearly reached the newspapers – a suggestion that she had moved her ball from a bad lie in the semi-final round.'

There are smaller worlds within golf based upon prejudice and social elitism. It can pollute with its pesticides and fertilizers. It can appropriate vast amounts of water and land from scarce resources. A Mallorcan friend of mine once said to me, 'The descendants of our farmers and artisans have learned servility as waiters. Our unharvested almond and olive trees have become tourist attractions. We have almost no water but we have more than twenty-five golf courses, even though Mallorcans don't play golf. Do you know anyone in Ireland who would know how to blow up golf courses?'

But golf is also healthy. It acquaints one with nature, or at least with some highly husbanded version of nature. It can be ecologically beneficial. It promotes comradeship. It is inclusive. It is a game at which the weak can have an even chance to defeat the strong. This is because of handi-capping. Handicapping is not a favour bestowed patronizingly by the better player on the poorer one. It is scientifically arrived at and intrinsically part of the game.

Arnold Palmer thinks that golf can help to promote world peace. Who knows? I don't, certainly. But it can at least be said that it is a non-violent sport in which civility and generosity are paramount and dishonesty is a disgrace. When Bobby Jones was congratulated for calling a penalty on himself for his ball having moved in the rough after he addressed it, even though no one saw it happen and even though it could be said to have cost him victory in the US Open, he replied, 'You may as well congratulate a man for not robbing a bank.' It is a game in which mind and body must work together in the most subtle of relationships, in which you are solely and manifestly accountable for what you have done, and in which you must strive to bear your hardships and your victories gracefully – though whether the spread of it can help make for a worse or better world I cannot say.

IV

Estrangement

I LIVED IN EXILE FROM GOLF THROUGHOUT MOST
of the 1970s. I played probably no more than a
dozen times during my four years at university.
Two weeks after leaving there I went to live on a
deserted island in Donegal, in the north-west of
Ireland. There was a nine-hole course in the dunes
on the mainland and I played a round there among
grazing sheep with a set of borrowed clubs that
looked as if they'd passed years leaning against
the wall of a barn. I was in the town one afternoon
buying food and I saw a young woman with long
thick dark hair and a face for the ages sitting in a
beam of sunlight on the ledge of the post office
window. I met her that night in a pub with a
racket of jigs and reels and Republican ballads
around us, and then she and the couple she was
travelling with came out to my little house on the
island. Her name was Teresa. She left her shoes
behind and I posted them to her.

I moved to Dublin when the cold autumn winds

made life on the island no longer possible. I had the idea of going back to Donegal in the winter to try to get work on the herring boats, but before that I went over to London to visit Teresa. She worked in a bank there and lived in a compact little room in Shepherd's Bush that looked out onto an enormous tree in the back garden and had a cooker and a blow heater and lots of books and records but no refrigerator. I stayed with her there for four years before we moved north- and eastwards across the city. We had a baby after a while, Aoife. I never worked on the fishing boats nor lived in Ireland nor, apart from a few months, in the United States again. I got a job at a cash register assembly factory and then worked for a while for a left-inclining publisher. I was made redundant there in the midst of a struggle to get the union recognized. Teresa and I went to sessions where accordionists and fiddlers played and acted in plays at an Irish theatre in the back of a pub in Islington. I wrote overwrought stories that were full of posturing and lacked authenticity. This went on for years. I wondered whether I would ever write a sentence in which I could believe.

Many things interested me while I waited nervously for the words to take form and strike me. I knew I could wait indefinitely, but what if the words never arrived? I lived in the shadow of that. But I stayed on the move. I had the impression of living a crowded life into which golf did not fit. My parents brought my clubs over on one of their annual visits from Chicago and I played some terrible rounds at public courses I could reach by bus or train. Golf still meant something to me. I remember the sudden feeling of elation I had when I read that Arnold Palmer had won tournaments in Canada and France late in his career. In theatres and cathedrals I would look up and wonder what club I would need to reach the upper gallery or the dome. But I no longer identified with golf in the way that I had. It had once been my principal form of self-expression and now no longer was. I played sometimes, but had ceased to think of myself as a golfer. I could not get a picture in my mind of the person I then thought I was, and then transplant with ease and clarity that person onto a golf course.

At some point during this period my father met Chick Evans and Chick asked him how I was and whether I was still playing golf. My father replied that I was fine but that I was playing very little as I was over in London without a car and without easy access to a course. I don't know in what manner this information was conveyed, but Chick was sufficiently moved by it to try to intervene. He wrote an open letter to the club secretaries of British golf clubs and had it delivered to my father, who then sent it on to me. The letterhead has a photograph of Chick in a golf hat surrounded by his trophies, and running down the left-hand margin is a list of some of his more important victories. The letter reads,

May 16, 1977

TO WHOMEVER IT MAY CONCERN:

I am taking the liberty, hoping my memories of seeing and playing many of the wonderful courses in Great Britain, of asking courtesies for the son of my outstanding Dentist whose name is Timothy E. O'Grady, 16 Bolingbroke Road, West Kensington, London W14, England.

The splendid father seems to think that his son has some depression due to his not being able to play his favorite game of golf.

I have enjoyed so many extremely fine friendships with British golfers and Clubs that I am emboldened to ask a great favor helping arrange for him to have a course to play on every once in awhile. I think Timothy has put an unreal value on all this.

Anything you can do for him will be a great kindness to me and a great compliment. I assure you that I will look for my time of reciprocity for trespassing on your valuable time.

I do hope Timothy can have some restrictions removed so that he can put his happiness trying to hit that uncertain ball.

Hopefully and gratefully yours,

Charles Evans Jr.

In its depiction of a morbidity induced by a drought of golf I think the letter does not quite catch the person I then was, but it nevertheless startled me. Chick Evans reached the highest point of American amateur golf by winning the US Amateur twice, once in the same year that he won the US Open. That was in 1916. No one had ever done that before, and the only person to do it afterwards was Bobby Jones in 1930, the year of his Grand Slam. Harry Vardon, who had been defeated by the young American amateur Francis Ouimet in the 1913 US Open, said that Chick was the best amateur he had played with in America. Jerry Travers, who won the US Amateur four times, said that 'if Evans could putt like Walter J. Travis it would be foolish to stage an Amateur tourney in this country.' It was like having W. H. Auden petition on your behalf for a pass to the British Library.

I hadn't a regular job for six years after I stopped working for the publisher. I worked for a while for the literary magazine *Transatlantic*

Review. I copyedited manuscripts for London publishers. I moved furniture and worked in a box office. I wrote a history book called *Curious Journey: An Oral History of Ireland's Unfinished Revolution*. The book was published and I still feel well towards it, but I did not think it meant I had written a sentence in which I could believe, because none of the sentences was fiction. I sat in libraries and continued to write stories badly.

When the London Festival Ballet came to the Festival Hall for their summer and Christmas seasons in the late 1970s, I worked as a stagehand. I was a flyman on the off-prompt side. The entire crew was brought together only for those seasons and when they weren't on they did other things to make their livings. There was a short, round, bearded impresario who imported Balinese dancers. There was a landscape gardener who had a doctorate in French colonial history. Two of the men in the wings worked on the shop floor of a furniture factory in the Caledonian Road. A propsman was having an affair with a ballerina and I think I had an oblique offer from one of them myself once, but I didn't take it up. Most of the dancers looked at us as though we were pieces of scenery.

On my fly floor there were two others apart from myself – an aesthete who'd read English at Oxford and subsequently sold wine, and a tall, bearded former student of astrophysics at Cambridge named Brian, who'd lived for a while in Hong Kong and seemed to have acquired a curiously Chinese look. He did *Times* crosswords on gantries high above the stage and invented complex machines with cranks and pulleys for flying the dancers off. He was also a golfer.

It was through Brian that I began to re-enter the game. Sometimes after working through the night to get the show set up a group of us would go for a pint in a Smithfield Market pub and then head to Richmond Park for a round of golf. I played appallingly. I'd swing so hard I'd nearly leave my feet and then top the ball to the front of the tee. We continued these games sporadically and there was a small improvement. I think I had a couple of reasonable scores at a nine-hole course in Dorking, where I remember eagling a par four after driving the green, perhaps twice. A first violin and another musician in the ballet's orchestra challenged Brian and me to a round at Royal Mid-Surrey, an old club that at one point draws near to the pagoda in Kew Gardens and on that day seemed to be full of retired senior civil servants and generals. I wore combat boots and torn jeans. Ridiculous, even if it was all I had available. Still, neither our host nor the venerable men in wicker chairs on the veranda made a comment. I hit a few good shots. I remember a four wood to the green that I could not have wished to improve upon. But mostly it was wretched. Nevertheless, Brian pulled us through and we won the match.

These games with the stagehands left me with a mournful yearning for golf. I began taking an overground train from Hackney Downs out to a course in Chingford. I met a man named John Collins there, a council estate caretaker who grew up in Mile End when it was dominated by the Kray twins. He and I and some of his friends played another round or two at Chingford and then moved across to the 36-hole layout at Hainault, where we played early Sunday-morning rounds on the lower course with the odd outing during the week. I liked this course better than any other I'd yet played around London. It was wooded and hilly. It had only one par five, but there were some excellent par fours, particularly six and twelve. I'd get picked up at dawn, we'd play for a few pounds and then we'd have fried eggs in the café after.

These men were older than me and relatively new to the game, but a couple of them played hard, particularly a half-Zulu, half-Irish park attendant named Vince. There was a Lothario named John who drove a minicab by day and did Frank Sinatra impersonations in East End pubs at night and once brought one of his girlfriends out onto the course with him. We'd been hearing about her activities for weeks and now there she was, twenty years younger than him, following him with wounded devotion while he concentrated on his game. There was an ex-boxer who'd had something of a career as a welterweight, but had the misfortune to coincide with the era of John Stracey. The club looked like a little twig in his hands. He could very occasionally hit the ball enormous distances but he liked to call me 'The Gorilla' whenever I caught a drive well. Taxi drivers played there, as did stallholders from the Ridley Road market in Dalston. You'd see Ford shiftworkers from the Dagenham plant with poor swings who played off five because their timing was so good after years of daily golf. The people I played with were thrilled to have discovered golf. They thought it should be kept a secret because if everyone knew how wonderful it was all the courses would be overwhelmed.

I finally found a sentence and wrote it down and then kept writing for four and a half years until I had a novel, which I called *Motherland*. I retreated again from golf during that time. I had a couple of jobs, there was the book, and then in the last months of writing it I had the operation on my back. I sat up in my bed on the ward when the others were asleep and kept on writing. I played my first round of golf after recuperating at

Ruislip, west London, with the writer Caryl Phillips. On the first hole I hit a drive down the right side, knocked a short iron up onto the green about forty feet past the hole and then rolled in the putt for a birdie. This is the kind of thing that golf feeds you before kneeing you in the groin.

In the absence of playing I talked about golf, if I found someone sufficiently sympathetic. But I was becoming aware that this was not so easy. I often got the idea that many people I met around London felt that golf was something about which one should be embarrassed, like having brass rubbing as a hobby, or being a Freemason, that it was solely for the crass, the pampered, the vulgarly aspirant. This surprised me. Golf was a game. You could be mesmerized by it, as I was, or indifferent towards it, but I didn't understand why anyone would allocate a portion of their energy to despising it. Animals weren't killed in it, or at least that was not its purpose. People were not maimed.

Perhaps the charge of snobbery is more readily to hand in a country like England, with its acute sensitivity to the gradations of class. This hadn't been my experience. All my golfing life I had been playing with people of different ages, races and levels of income on cheap, municipal courses. I thought that golf, which allowed for competition as equals by players of all abilities, was the most democratic and open of sports. I had met a far wider variety of people through golf than I had through, for example, education or drinking in pubs. It is very unlikely that I would have known the men I played with at Hainault had it not been for golf. Golf creates friendships that would otherwise be unlikely to exist. It was not that I was unaware that there were snobs who played golf. I had worked at a private club. I knew that many private clubs, perhaps most, were closed off from the world, were full of infantile prejudices and were designed to make their members feel that they ruled their countries, or at least their little patches of them. But would anyone judge third-level education by an Oxford high table, or public houses by the bar at Claridge's? Golf is as much for the Glasgow postman on the bus with his clubs as it is for the corporate executive.

And the clubs are not necessarily as they may superficially seem, particularly the older and more traditional. They are made for an elite but they nevertheless abhor ostentation. The members sit around in the bar in their dun-coloured golf attire like schoolboys in uniforms, privileged collectively but equal among themselves. Displays of wealth or personal importance have a rank odour. They can result in ostracization. This ethos is embodied in the club secretary, an employee but also a disciplinarian and custodian of the codes. My accountant told me that one day at Ganton in Yorkshire a white Rolls-Royce advanced up the driveway in front of the clubhouse and parked next to a sign which said 'No Parking'. Two men wearing suits got out of the car. They were smoking cigars. They walked across the lawn past a sign which read 'Please do not walk on the grass'. The club secretary was standing on the clubhouse steps with a clipboard with the day's starting times in his hand, looking at them out of narrowed eyes. The men stopped in front of him.

'Are you the caddy master?' they asked.

'That's right, men,' said the club secretary, 'and we have no need of caddies today.'

I also encountered around London the idea that golf could hardly be thought of as a sport, that it was something between bowls and rambling, but less demanding and more artificial than either. A person who has not played golf could not reasonably be expected to know of the enormous labour that goes into playing it well, of the infinitesimally precise degree of coordination and control required, of the mental and physical endurance demanded by tournament play. But then nor should such people expect to be free to pronounce judgement on it. Several of the people I met making these and other charges were book reviewers, journalists and other media and public relations people, or actresses just back from a yoga class. Many fitted the privileged, elitist, socially and materially aspirant prototypes that they attacked golf for harbouring, though they went about their aspiring in a different style. Behind this charge that golf was not a sport was the idea that it was a game for sissies, or for those too old and unfit to do anything else. So confident were they in making this charge that one would think they passed their spare time bullfighting or sparring with Oscar de la Hoya. William Hazlitt was repeatedly abused for his enthusiasm for boxing, which he called 'the Fancy', and, articulate as he was about so many things, had this to say in reply: 'Ye who despise the Fancy, do something to show as much pluck, or as much self-possession as this, before you assume a superiority which you have never given a single proof of by any one action in the whole of your lives.' I only came upon this recently. I wish I had known it earlier.

What they are saying is that golf is uncool. They don't like the clothes. They don't like the physiques. It is played by the old, the fat, the suburban, the unglamorous. It is played by provincial Rotarians wishing to increase their business contacts and confirm their social status.

But golf is wider than that. Machinists, security guards, lorry drivers and hookers are golfers. Ghetto residents and jazz singers. Michael

Jordan, Hurricane Higgins and Ivan Lendl play golf. Oscar de la Hoya as well, as it happens. Joe Louis played and ran his own tournament in Detroit for black professionals. Samuel Beckett played a kind of minimalist golf using only four clubs yet attained a handicap of seven. He was an insomniac and when asked what he did to try to get to sleep replied, 'I play in my mind the first nine holes of the Carrickmines Golf Club near Dublin, and if that doesn't work I play the back nine as well.' Robert Graves played with Siegfried Sassoon. The Irish novelist Aidan Higgins set a course record in Wicklow. Rudyard Kipling learned golf from Arthur Conan Doyle and painted his golf balls red so he could play in the snow when he was living in New England. Anthony Trollope used to bellow his way around the course. He once collapsed onto the green in grief over a missed putt but then immediately sprang up again yelping in pain as he had landed on a golf ball in his pocket. Cormac McCarthy is evidently so captivated by the game that he determines whether or not to accept invitations to readings according to their proximity to golf courses. Meatloaf, Madonna and Sharon Stone all play. Jack Nicholson is a single handicap player. Alice Cooper has played off four and advertises Calloway golf clubs on American television. Willie Nelson owns a course called Pedernales in

Texas. Dennis Hooper played with him there when he was making *The Texas Chainsaw Massacre Part 2* and said about it: 'The dress code there was like men could basically wear anything, but they'd prefer them to keep their pants on. Women, they didn't care, but they'd prefer them not to keep their pants on.' Hopper started to play golf in order to have something to do when he became sober, but had difficulty finding a club which would accept him, as, he said, had Victor Mature many years before when he applied to the Los Angeles Country Club. 'We're sorry, Mr Mature,' they said, 'but we don't accept actors here.' 'Actors?' said Mature. 'Nobody's ever accused me of being an actor before.' Hopper was finally accepted at Riviera, but continued to play in a threeball with Neil Young and Bob Dylan at a Japanese-owned public course near Malibu. Young, whose brother is a professional, is a good player and once competed in a tournament organized by Eddie van Halen. Dylan, too, is reputed to play a respectable game. 'He's sort of taken it up,' says Hopper. Iggy Pop evidently plays well enough to have given lessons to Lou Reed. Joe Pesci and Samuel L. Jackson play, as do numerous professional snooker, cricket, basket-ball, ice hockey, rugby, baseball and football players. Che Guevara played as a young man in Argentina and again later in combat fatigues on a course in Cuba after the revolution. Probably not many book reviewers play. They may fear the exposure.

Some of those who have played have also written about it. In 1743 Thomas Mathison wrote a long poem in cantos called *The Goff: An Heroi-Comical Poem*, in which Castalio vanquishes Pygmalion on the final green by knocking in a shot 'full fifteen clubs' lengths from the hole'. Tobias Smollett watched a group of golfers on the links at Leith, the youngest of whom was eighty and who, he said, 'had amused themselves with this pastime for the best part of a century, without ever having felt the least alarm from sickness or disgust; and they never went to bed without having each the best part of a gallon of claret in his belly'. Arthur Balfour, the prime minister, wrote perceptively about golf. John Betjeman wrote a poem about birdieing the thirteenth hole at St Enodoc which includes the lines 'A glorious, sailing, bounding drive/That made me glad I was alive'. William Faulkner played, and began *The Sound and the Fury* with the sentence, 'Through the fence, between the curling flower spaces, I could see them hitting.' Ford Madox Ford, Ian Fleming, A. A. Milne, Julian Barnes, George MacDonald Fraser, Walker Percy, Richard Ford and Damon Runyon have all written about golf. John Updike has written enough articles, stories and parts of novels about golf to form a collection which he called *Golf Dreams*. He is particularly eloquent on bad shots. But P. G. Wodehouse, I think, must be judged supreme among writers of golf fiction. His collection of stories about the Oldest Living Member runs to nearly five hundred pages. 'There were three things in the world that he held in the smallest esteem –' wrote Wodehouse in his story 'Rodney Fails to Qualify', 'slugs, poets, and caddies with hiccups.'

'Golf converts oddly well into words,' wrote Updike. Metaphors seem bountiful concerning the flight of the ball, or a player's reaction to it. Golf lends itself to allegory, for each round is so manifestly a journey, and to comedy because it is played with such intense seriousness.

I got my first opportunity to write about golf in 1991 when a friend of mine working for *Esquire* magazine in London phoned me to say that they were preparing a supplement about golf and asked if I would like to contribute to it. For my first assignment I went north to the Dunlop-Slazenger club and ball manufacturing works in Normanton, West Yorkshire to watch a robot called Metal Max test clubs and balls on their driving range. Metal Max could hit drives further than John Daly if programmed to do so. The day I was there he was hitting low, Lee Trevino-like fades.

Writing about golf was eventually to get me to wonderful and very expensive courses I would certainly never otherwise have played, and brought me into contact with people I would never otherwise have met. I had a conversation with Jose Maria Olazabal for an hour in his hotel room in Malaga. Afterwards he let me swing his three iron out on the lawn. I said that I had hoped we could play a round together but as this had not been possible perhaps we could imagine it. 'Fine,' he said. 'How are we doing?' 'I'm three up after fourteen,' I said. He feigned shock. 'I must go to the practice tee,' he said. I had another hour with Tom Watson on the lawn in front of the club-house at Royal St George's at the British Open in the year that he captained the American Ryder Cup team.

But the most pleasing thing of all about writing about golf was the unexpected sensation of this game so thwarting in the playing seeming to convert 'oddly well into words'. I was pleased, and grateful, finally to be writing fiction after fearing for more than ten years that I might never do it. But it was incomparably the hardest thing I had ever attempted to do. A normal day involved three hours of walking around a small room and staring at its walls, followed by a staggering run of a few hundred words, several or all of which might be excised the next or some other day. There is an inchoate idea existing somewhere in your consciousness that has a sufficient urgency about it to make you want to express it, and then in another place is such knowledge and sense of form and capacity to name as you might possess. You try to bring them all into alignment. You do this with each sentence and each sentence is done blind. It is an act of controlled abandon, like a golf swing, except that unlike a golf swing each sentence is unrepeatable. You are forever entering this idea, or attempting to enter it, and then leaving it, and at any point you could enter by the wrong door. You might never enter by the right door. You are never free of anxiety. You live with the fear of insufficiently serving the idea which has somehow been given you. Such, at least, has been my experience. But writing about golf, I found, was utterly different. I had a good time doing it. It felt simple, fluid, natural. I'd felt many things writing fiction, including, very rarely, excitement. But I'd never felt easeful pleasure. Writing about golf had that – an easeful pleasure. I'd get to the end of a day and be disinclined to stop. I had the feeling I could go on doing it around the clock. It never involved those grinding, mind-splitting efforts at concentration which make you eager to flee the task. It just seemed to roll out. There was a feeling in this of liberation.

V

Professionals

MY FATHER TOLD ME THAT ANY ILLUSIONS HE might momentarily have harboured about there being only a narrow margin of difference between a good amateur and a professional were broken for ever by a single shot struck during a round he played in California. The shot was made by a touring professional who had once won the US PGA Championship. I don't remember his name, or the reason why my father was playing with him. The pro had had an injury and was just then beginning gently to play his way back into the game after a period of recuperation. His play was a little erratic. On one hole he hit a drive way out to the right onto an adjacent fairway. He was around two hundred yards away from the green with a line of high trees blocking his route all the way. He took out a mid-iron and hit it straight down the line of the fairway he had landed on, parallel to the hole he was meant to be playing. My father did not understand the idea of this shot until somewhere near the apex of the ball's trajectory, when it suddenly turned directly left in the air like one of those toy cars directed by remote control panels, swinging some forty yards over the trees at a sharp angle to its previous line of flight before dropping gently onto the green. My father had never seen a shot like that before. He could hit draws and fades in varying parabolic arcs, but he had never imagined a ball could be made to behave in the way he had just seen. He knew that no matter how many times the shot's execution was explained to him and how much effort he devoted to practising it, he would never be able to hit it. He had good hands, but his hands could not be made to do that.

I had a similar experience when playing with a club pro named Doug Wood at the Jasper Park course in the Canadian Rockies. I was travelling in a large group and one morning, when the others were hungover, he and I went out early and played at a blinding lick, the whole of the eighteen holes in two hours and something. 'This is what it's all about,' Doug said as we galloped between shots. He was spending most of his time selling sweaters in his shop at Banff and his game was a little ragged. He was beating me, but not by a lot. There is a wonderful par four at Jasper Park, the fourteenth, set down beside a lake, the hole doglegging left along the shoreline. Elk were strolling around behind the tee when we got there. We both hit our second shots right of the green, behind a line of low shrubs, too close to try to pop the ball over. 'We're stymied, Doug,' I said to him. 'There's no such thing as a stymie,' he said and took out a wedge, hooded it a little and rolled his wrists over at impact. It was a little chip and run shot and he *hooked* it, the ball actually bending left slightly around the shrub even though it was airborne for no more than forty feet. It took a hard left kick when it hit the edge of the green because of all the spin he'd put on it and then ran down to about four feet from the hole. I'd stood behind him to watch the shot and when he'd done it I wondered whether it was somehow an optical illusion, something to do with the water and the lie of the land. I wondered too whether he'd got the left kick because the ball had hit a bump on the fringe of the green. But when I looked at all the different angles I found that the shot must have worked as I had originally perceived it. It was all spin. If someone had told me about this shot I'd have had great difficulty believing it.

A good pro will beat an amateur in almost every instance. Pros make a higher percentage of solid strikes, they have more shots available to them with each club, their misses are less catastrophic, they're better around the greens and they think better. They have a good idea of the percentage of risk with each shot, and they know what to do with this knowledge. They have both an empirical and an intuitive sense of when to lay back and when to turn on the power, and play most of the time well within their capacities. They tend not to unravel after an atrocious shot or hole. Each knows with scientific exactitude his own game in all its many varieties and has several ways of salvaging a poor situation and exploiting a good one. An English pro told me that he's placed respectably in tournaments in which he was badly out of rhythm by hitting each full shot half strength. 'It was embarrassing,' he said. 'But I was able to make good scores.' The entire demeanour of professionals from the time they get out of their cars to the moment they put their clubs away is different from the amateur's. You can see their skill, their confidence, their intimacy with the game in the methodical way they go about their work, their familiarity with their instruments, the way their gestures and their gait and their swings are all of a piece rhythmically. There is a silence about them, a slowness, an authoritative calmness. They appear self-sufficient.

Perhaps all athletes have this. I saw the same look on the faces of a line of bullfighters in the lobby of a hotel in Bilbao. They were still, passive, calm and imposing. Perhaps the ability to express oneself at the highest level physically obviates the fretful urgency to express oneself through spoken words. Musicians have this too, I have noticed, once they reach a certain level. Words can be serviceable, pleasant or entertaining, but they are not the principal form of expression for them. They have become redundant.

But what distinguishes a great professional, a multiple winner of major championships, from a good one? What constitutes the journey he makes? I can only guess. Many are gifted athletically and excelled when young at other sports. This would suggest an innate agility, strength, good hand–eye coordination and competitiveness. Perhaps too an instinctive grasp of the body's dynamics. Jack Nicklaus was an excellent basketball player. Babe Zaharias was an Olympic champion in athletics and Patty Berg was a speed skater. Sam Snead, Walter Hagen and Raymond Floyd seriously considered professional baseball careers. Paul McGinley, who may never win a major championship but who will for ever be remembered for his putt on the eighteenth at the Belfry to win the 2002 Ryder Cup, was a fine Gaelic football player. Some have unusual physical attributes. There must be something peculiar going on in John Daly's wrists that makes it possible for him to get the club pointing down at the ground at the top of his backswing, or in Sergio Garcia's that he hits the ball so late. Sam Snead, even in advanced years, could kick the ceiling of a bar from a standing position for a bet. He had the most admired swing in all of golf – 'the most fluid, natural and authentic', as Arnold Palmer described it. He was said to be 'double-jointed', but he said his joints were just unusually loose.

Almost all the great players entered the game when very young, practised to the point of exhaustion and quickly became prodigious – eerily so in the case of Tiger Woods. There is a story told to a journalist by Tiger's father about him proposing to a local pro that he play a match with his gifted son. If Tiger won he was to be granted free playing privileges at the pro's course. The only stipulations were that Tiger play from the ladies' tees and be given a shot per hole. The pro agreed, they went out on the course and Tiger won the match. 'His age?' asked the journalist of Earl Woods. 'Four,' he replied. Earl Woods was obsessed by golf, but was not particularly skilled at it. Many fine players have fathers who were pros – David Duval, Davis Love III, Sergio Garcia, Arnold Palmer. Palmer said that his father set him up with the basic grip, stance and swing plane and then said, 'Now hit it hard, go find it and hit it hard again.' 'I never managed to hit it quite hard enough to please him,' said Palmer.

Great talent, I think, generates the will to bring that talent to fruition. As talent develops so does will, and as will develops so does talent. The two come to feed off each other. If a person has a singing voice sent down from the heavens, that person is likely to have a fascination with that voice, will look for all number of ways to give it depth, nuance and authenticity and finally will go anywhere and do anything, including in some cases walking over the backs of those who are in their way, in order for that voice to be heard. It is only a stillborn thing unless it is sent out into the world. There is an impression held by some that genius is a delicate and unworldly thing, that such is the power and originality of its products that the world doesn't know how to receive them and that therefore many masterpieces lie unknown in drawers or in attics. I think this unlikely. Genius tends to demand to be heard. It creates its own hard skin, and capacity for endurance. James Joyce promulgated the myth of the lofty, detached artist, but when his first book was rejected more than forty times he kept on until it found a home. Such was his self-belief. This might also be called ambition, thought by many to be an ugly thing. But among the greatest of artists, as among the greatest of golfers, it is generally not an ambition for money or fame or to grind others underfoot – though it may be an ambition for immortality. It is more to do with completing the act that began with the self-discovery of the skill, in the case of the golfer, or of the idea, in the case of the artist, of expressing oneself and having that expression received by the world. 'A skill unexpressed is an anguish,' I read somewhere – skill as an athlete, a doctor, an artist, a lover. But a skill expressed is an exuberance. When I interviewed Tom Watson he said, 'I was silent much of the time when I was young. Even the thought of speaking to people I didn't know was something I found paralysing. But golf was something through which I discovered I could express myself and establish my presence, be somehow acknowledged in the world.'

Self-expression is onanistic without someone receiving it. You can sense this in the face of a child struggling with words, the fervid need to reach another person and be understood. The drive to do this, I believe, is as profound and elemental as the will to survive. It is the depth and intensity of this drive that makes the difference between the good and the great. Arnold Palmer was asked what he thought his greatest strength as a player had been. Year after year golf magazines judged him the best long-iron player in the game. He was renowned for his power, his attacking play, his ability to escape from trouble and his fearless putting. But his answer included none of these things. 'Desire,' he said.

Talent and desire are often first made visible through the devotion to practice. Sylvia Plath wrote one thousand villanelles during one of her summer holidays from university. Jimi Hendrix is known to have wandered around for days with his guitar, ceaselessly plucking it. Golf professionals practise in a way that seems to reach the borderlands of mania and for amounts of hours unequalled in other sports. Vijay Singh is said to practise for eight hours per day. When Walter Hagen was a boy he built his own four-hole course in a cow pasture and was in it through the whole of the day. When he was at university, Jack Nicklaus could be seen hitting balls into a field long into the night, lit by the headlamps of his father's car. Ben Hogan hit six hundred balls every day before lunch and then played in the afternoon. He believed that if he took two or three days off he would feel the negative effect for up to three months.

There is no player, to my knowledge, who has reached the heights of the game without at some early point in his life hitting balls all day and every day for a considerable period. Severiano Ballesteros is a player thought to have excelled through inspiration, feel and a celestially bestowed swing. He went out onto the beach at Pedrena with his three iron as a child and his golf was thereafter sustained by the pure magic of his being. Such is the myth. I saw him practise at Malaga. He arrived from Dubai having just won a tournament. He warmed up on the practice ground for forty-five minutes and then played eighteen holes with four balls on every hole. He gave a press conference, had lunch and then went back to the practice ground for three hours to hit high, drawn four irons, a shot he was working on for Augusta. He pitched and chipped for half an hour and then joined the other pros on the putting green. One by one they left. Finally even his caddy left. It was dark. He stayed alone for nearly another hour practising his putting in the spill of the dining-room lights through the clubhouse window.

Practising in this way can seem from the outside to be tedious, gruelling, even physically painful. But I think the professionals themselves, at least the best of them, find it fascinating. Ben Hogan's practice regime was thought by some to be a kind of self-flagellation. But he loved it. 'I couldn't wait to get up in the morning and hit golf balls,' he said. Everyone's game is in flux, but only good players are acutely sensitive to this and know how to correct and evolve. They practise in order to correct flaws, to tune their timing and tempo, to instil a workable swing deeply in the memory of the muscles so that it will repeat even under the most trying of circumstances, but also,

I think, to get close to the unreachable heart of the game. 'I am waiting for the day when everything falls into place,' said Tom Watson, 'when everything makes sense, when every swing is with confidence and every shot is exactly what I want. I know it can be done. I've been close enough to smell it a couple of times, but I'd like to touch it, to feel it. I know it's been touched. Hogan touched it. Byron Nelson touched it. Then I think I could be satisfied. Then I think I could walk away from the game.' But really there is no point at which the process ends. This is one of the great strengths of golf. I once met a woman in Soho in London, then a painter and still very beautiful in her forties, who twenty years earlier had worked in an escort bar and earned more than any of the other girls because she wouldn't sleep with the customers. Golf ultimately derives its power and mystique from this same force – it is both everlastingly inviting and everlastingly inviolable.

Idolatry has set many on their way to greatness. Pinter revered Beckett as Bob Dylan revered Woody Guthrie. Bobby Jones motivated the young Jack Nicklaus as subsequently Nicklaus motivated the young Nick Faldo. The spectacle of greatness is thrilling, alluring, intoxicating. It can make the beholder want to do the same thing, breathe the same air. In the case of the young golfer, if the interest has been ignited and the skill developed and displayed and the decision finally made to become a touring professional, what stands between him and the achievements of his hero? There are the other players, of course, around 150 of the world's best at every major championship. Even at a minor event on a satellite tour the practice ground is full of players with swings of repetitive, metronomic simplicity hitting shot after shot of apparent perfection. There are the technical flaws in one's game – something unreliable in the swing, erratic putting, wild driving. Even Jack Nicklaus was said to be weak with the wedge, one of the most important clubs in the bag along with the putter and the driver.

But most of what will impede a promising young player has to do with the mind's resistance to assuming the forms and manners needed for the winning of a championship. A player must learn to contend with the loneliness and anonymity of life lived perpetually on the road. He must learn to silence his mind, cauterize his emotions and make his body robotic, unnatural though such things are. He is both a player and a businessman, and he must find a way of relating to the making of money that does not interfere with his playing. Money can be scarce for a player struggling to qualify for the tour, but not so many years ago it was scarce for nearly all touring professionals, particularly in Europe. Now there is so much money in golf through sponsorship and prize money even for players halfway down the money list that money in itself no longer provides the kind of win-or-starve motivation that drove Snead, Hogan and Lee Trevino. Leading players are pampered wherever they go. They are surrounded by people whose incomes depend on serving and flattering them. The mind gets softened by luxury, the senses dulled by corporate drinks parties where players must talk with people they are likely to feel no affinity towards. To be great they must maintain the simple, vigorous and impassioned relationship with the game they began with. They must in the most fundamental way stay humble before it, as a musician must be humble towards his music or a writer towards language, for the game is of course more powerful than they are and if they approach it with smugness they will play it poorly. Yet this is not easy. Money and flattery, the endless selling of oneself and answering of the same tedious questions can sour a player's taste for the game. It can make it seem burdensome and artificial.

The young pro must also find a way of contending with anger, because he will almost certainly feel it. Golf is an enraging game. Bobby Jones said that when he played in his first US

Amateur he and his opponent threw clubs so often that from behind they looked like a juggling act. Arnold Palmer threw a club over a tree in a school championship and was told by his father that if he did it again he would no longer be allowed to play. Both Jones and Palmer found ways of controlling themselves, but certain others didn't. Tommy Bolt advised throwing one's club in the direction of the shot so that you could pick it up on the way. Lefty Stackhouse, an American touring pro of the 1930s and '40s, knocked himself out with a punch to the jaw after a missed putt. He once threw himself into a rosebush and thrashed around until he came out looking, as Dave Marr said, like he'd 'fought a bunch of wildcats in a small room', and on another occasion after a poor round went out to the parking lot and destroyed his car, tearing off the windshield and doors and hurling around pieces of the engine. A contemporary of his named Ky Laffoon became so infuriated with his putter while driving from one tournament to another that he tied it to his door handle and watched it bounce along the road. More recently Jose Maria Olazabal broke his hand punching a hotel room wall at the US Open after a round that displeased him. Players try to find ways of absorbing it. It's destructive, embarrassing, commercially negative and intrusive to other players.

Tom Watson follows the path of a badly hit shot until the ball comes to a halt – partly to punish himself by taking in its complete awfulness but also to slow himself down and prevent himself from rushing after the ball and doing the same again. Ballesteros has deprived himself of meals after bad rounds. 'You don't deserve to eat,' he would tell himself. Most players eventually learn to control at least the most excessive expressions of rage out of a sense of dignity and politeness towards others, and to prevent unravelling and protect concentration. It is difficult, and can be a slow process. Raymond Floyd thinks that the main reason most players don't enter their primes until their thirties is that it takes that long to find a way of dealing with anger.

But more treacherous mentally than anything else is the pressure of competitive golf. All tournaments are the stories not of a few hours but of nearly an entire week, and major tournaments in particular are a long haul, certainly among the most arduous experiences in sport. The best players build their year around them. The courses are all extremely severe. A fifteen-handicapper playing a course set up for a championship from the back tees would be unlikely to break one hundred once in twenty attempts. On Augusta's greens during Masters week such a player would, as Peter Alliss has suggested, probably average four putts per hole. The player knows that everyone has to play the same course, but he also knows that a single errant shot can send him crashing down the leaderboard. The atmosphere at a major championship is intense and vibrant and full of significance. You can feel it up to a mile away as you approach the course. In this atmosphere the player is utterly alone. He is unable to hide. He has no one to blame should there be a catastrophe. He fears degrading himself, not only before those immediately around him but also in front of millions watching on television around the world. Golf, like snooker, another game executed from a starting position of complete stillness, is extremely susceptible to pressure. The pressure is ever-present and increases inexorably if the player remains in contention. In golf the mind has ample time to fill with fear. Mind and body which were united when the play was good can fragment instantaneously into hundreds of component parts. The breath gets short, the muscles tighten, the mind cannot be stilled, the stomach turns. Bobby Jones regularly lost up to eighteen pounds in the course of a major championship. It is even worse in the Ryder Cup where to play badly is to risk not only loss and humiliation but also the grave dis-appointment of the captain, teammates and the continent of fans all of whose fates are bound up for those few days with the player's. Davis Love III had been warned about how extreme an assault on the nerves is playing in the Ryder Cup, but nothing prepared him for what he felt as he faced an ostensibly simple short-iron shot over water to the eighteenth green at the Belfry in 1993 when its failure or success would determine the outcome of the competition. 'I couldn't breathe,' he said. 'There was no saliva in my mouth. It took all my strength not to kneel down in the fairway and throw up on myself.' When Mark Calcavecchia lost the last four holes of his match to draw with Colin Montgomerie at Kiawah Island he had to be taken to a medical tent and given oxygen.

The first tee shot in a major competition can be a trauma, but the final few holes when the competition is close are of course many times worse. To finish well a long and difficult labour in which the self is pitilessly exposed takes a different dimension of strength from what has been required up to that point. The urge to flee is great and the ability to endure repeatedly in the face of this is another of the things that distinguishes the great players. It is the difference between Tom Wolfe bailing out before ending *The Bonfire of the Vanities* by contriving some newspaper reports to deal with the fates of his characters and, on the other hand, the magnificent and symphonic cascades of language with which James Joyce ended *Ulysses* and *Finnegans Wake*. He was at his best when the pressure was greatest and the stakes at their highest. Of the great major championship winners, Hogan, Nicklaus and, so far, Tiger Woods have been consistently strong at the close.

A good young player setting out on the tour will almost certainly face a long period of failure before he ever begins to win anything important. Perhaps this is the hardest of all the tests presented by professional golf to a player who has been accustomed to winning regularly as an amateur. Jack Nicklaus and Tiger Woods began winning immediately, but the more common story is Justin Rose's, who nearly won the British Open as an amateur and then missed his first twenty-one cuts as a pro.

Golf's apprenticeship is long, perhaps the longest in sport. Several of the greatest players laboured in near anonymity for a decade before entering their period of glory. Ben Hogan went on the tour in 1932 and did not win anything at all until 1940. He won his first major in 1946. Bobby Jones entered the US Open eleven times before he finally won it, his first major, in 1923. Chick Evans was a loser in the semi-finals of the US Amateur so often that he was moved to write a lyric about it:

I've a semi-final hoodoo, I'm afraid.
I can never do as you do, Jimmy Braid.
I've a genius not to do it,
I excel at almost to it,
But I never can go through it, I'm
    afraid.

He eventually got to the final in 1912 but was
crushed seven and six by Jerry Travers and was
so depressed he wandered off alone down a
country road with the noise of the celebration
party pouring from the clubhouse windows
behind him. After a long while he came to a barn
where he could hear music playing. There was a
square dance going on inside and he went in and
danced himself through the night into a state of
equanimity. But he still didn't win the championship until four years later. Tom Watson was
thought to have insufficient nerve to win a major
championship after collapses at the Masters and
US Open, but he eventually went on to win five
British Opens in nine years, as well as three other
majors, beating Jack Nicklaus toe to toe a few
times with Nicklaus playing at his best. There is
always someone in golf being asked the question,
'What does it feel like repeatedly to have failed to
win a major championship?'

A long apprenticeship can be demoralizing, but
it may also be necessary. A golfer almost certainly

97

must lose often in order to find the way to win. We learn to walk by failing. 'It takes ten years to learn how to write a sentence,' according to the novelist Charles Newman, and after ten years it remains an activity largely carried out in the dark, failure a kind of ghost accompanying a writer line by line, year after year. A sentence, like a golf shot, is nearly always a miss or approximation of some kind. A gifted young golfer turning pro may hit the ground running but he will almost always be felled brutally and repeatedly by the tour. He must learn hard lessons about what his weaknesses and strengths are and how to adapt to them, he must learn to think well, handle pressure and find a way to win. But no matter how good he is and how successful he is at learning these things he will still win rarely. Nicklaus in his best years won less than a quarter of the tournaments he entered. And even at the highest level the player fails with nearly every shot. 'Ever tried. Ever failed. No matter. Try again. Fail again. Fail better,' wrote Samuel Beckett, golfer and writer.

There finally comes the time when the great champion enters the era over which he will establish his ascendancy, when all the elements of his game come to fruition, when he displays those qualities of suppleness and courage and beauty which Solon praised in the first Olympic athletes. There are certain rounds, tournaments and occasionally seasons when a great golfer's play is definitive of the best of himself and his time, when he is untouchable and leaves all around him awed, when, as C. L. R. James wrote about Gary Sobers batting at Brisbane in 1961, 'He seemed to be expressing a personal vision.' In recent years, for example, there have been Ballesteros shooting sixty-five to beat Nick Price at Lytham in 1988, Greg Norman's final round at Sandwich in 1993, Tiger Woods at Augusta in 1997 or through the millennial season when he won three major championships. The mind in such cases seems entirely to possess the course and the game. The club feels light and the hole looks big. Time moves slowly. The path of the shot and the ball itself are vividly apprehended. The player feels strong, loose and balanced and walks as though buoyed on a cloud. He may not go so far as to say it to himself, but he believes innately that he cannot miss. He is free of worry, and of thought. There is a wonderful, easeful singularity and simplicity to it all, the ball rising from the heart of the club, the putts rolling in, the ball doing just as the player wishes it to do, over and over again.

Arnold Palmer described this feeling. 'When I was at my best I was always completely in the game. The concentration was automatic. Concentration comes out of a combination of confidence and desire. One year when I was still in college I entered the Azalea Open, which was a professional tournament down in North Carolina. I stayed with some friends of mine who had a cottage there and while we were having a few beers around the table the night before the tournament one of them asked me what I was going to do the next day. I was to be in a threeball with two of the top five money winners that year. I suppose I had cause to be nervous, but I felt well. I said to my friend, "I'll tell you what I'm going to do," and I went through the entire eighteen holes, shot by shot. He laughed and I laughed, but then I went to bed and dreamed it all over again, the whole round of golf. And when I played the next day I did exactly what I said I would. I shot sixty-five. I never came out of that feeling the whole way around. I *loved* it. It was the same with the last round of the US Open at Cherry Hills. I wasn't afraid of anything. I just saw where I wanted the ball to go and I put it there.'

The career of a champion has a trajectory which also has a downwards arc. Nicklaus's trajectory has been longer than anyone else's probably because his reserves of concentration were greater and because when he was younger he had the foresight to play well within himself and schedule his season so as not to leave himself exhausted. But of course for him too the point of no return has arrived. As he said himself when he was fifty-four, 'People have always said, "Jack, I wish I could play like you." Well, now they can.'

Usually a great player lasts no longer than six or eight years at the top of the game. Why should this be? Golf is not sprinting, or ju-jitsu. There is some diminishment in strength and stamina with age, but it is not sufficient to be of great significance in a sport where these characteristics are less prominent. Yet most dominant players have ceased to be dominant by the age of forty. Very often it's putting. Towards the end of his competitive career Bobby Jones used to stand over putts and hear the pounding of his heart like the beating of a Lambeg drum, his whole field of vision washed over as though with a red dye. Hogan came to loathe putting. He once said while walking towards the practice putting green at Augusta, 'And now for the bloodbank,' and eventually proposed that putting be eliminated from the game. As he got older he stood longer and longer over the ball on the greens, unable to move his hands. Tony Jacklin, Bernhard Langer and Tom Watson have all been traumatized by putting. The condition takes the form of paralysis and when finally the move is made to strike the putt the player has no control over or knowledge of what his hands, shoulders and head are doing. Some players suffer this anguish throughout their careers and therefore never win championships.

Wild Bill Melhorn was one of the great ball-strikers of the 1920s and '30s and once managed to shoot sixty-five in a competition while so drunk that he had to get his caddie to tee the ball for him so he wouldn't fall over. But he couldn't putt. He once six-putted in a tournament from ten feet. In another tournament he had a three-foot put to tie for the lead and after standing over it for a long time he whacked it off the green and into a bunker. One of his playing partners standing on the fringe of the green had to leap out of the way of the ball.

Arnold Palmer thinks that a champion's demise often has to do with fear. 'You become a victim of yourself,' he has said. 'You play with confidence and win major tournaments, but then you're like the big home-run hitter in baseball who hits sixty home runs one season and then the following spring on the first day of the season he looks at the pitcher and thinks, "Damn, I've got to hit sixty home runs again this year." He tries to protect what he's done, and the doubts come in, and maybe that year he only hits ten home runs. In golf you know you can play the game but you begin to think, "I've got to keep the ball on the fairway," or "I can't afford to three-putt." Where you used to attack, now you're protecting. It all just gets fed into the diet and you find you're not winning tournaments like you used to do. Whether you win again at all depends on how well you handle this. But nobody escapes it. It's like death. If you hang around long enough it's going to get you.'

No one's decline from the top of the game has been as precipitous as Severiano Ballesteros's. The man Peter Dobreiner described as 'the great matador of golf' now rarely makes a cut. He regularly hits shots that would shame a fifteen-handicapper. How has this happened? Like many professional golfers he has had trouble with his back. Perhaps too he now gives the greater part of himself to his family, and while the wish to win may remain, the deep need to do so does not. Certainly money can no longer motivate him as he has earned enough on his own to keep several succeeding generations, and also married into one of the richest families in Spain. It is also the case that he has listened to so much conflicting technical advice that he may in some way have short-circuited, for what was once the freest and most majestic swing in golf now appears hemmed in by paranoia. He himself speaks of bad and good golf in terms of mood, forces unknowable and beyond control, the good mood something that one can with all fervour and sincerity invite to come, but which never-theless moves mysteriously and capriciously. 'I had one mood from 1976 through 1986,' he has said, 'a mood of great confidence and optimism. I always felt aggressive, I always had a great deal of self-control, I always felt I would get good bounces. Then . . . I didn't feel so invincible. I was pessimistic. I believed that if something could go wrong, it would go wrong. I thought there was the devil in me. I said, "Where has the confidence gone? Where has the optimism gone?" It hadn't left me. It was *inside* me, but I couldn't bring it out.'

Ezra Pound believed that people are born with an allotted word hoard and because of this he stayed silent for long periods to conserve his words and thereby have some left to spend when he was old. Perhaps athletes each have a finitude of desire, and with each competitive effort they draw on this bank until the reserves are spent. In golf it could perhaps be said that Tom Weiskopf, for example, was granted a lesser amount of this than Jack Nicklaus. Ballesteros had two phases, or moods, of winning with élan and when he looked for a third it could not be found. Samuel Beckett yearned nostalgically for decades for that time of explosive production during which he wrote *Waiting for Godot* and *Endgame* and his trilogy of novels, writing all day and drinking all night, the supply of language seemingly never-ending. But it played itself out and the words came to him in diminishing numbers, something out of which he made an aesthetic in itself but which nevertheless became a kind of anguish, his hand, he said, drifting across the table towards his closed exercise book, stalling and then withdrawing without a word being recorded. If he succeeded in writing a sentence his mind would usually howl, 'That's a lie!'

Athletes, perhaps like women of great beauty, know that the period of their glory has a limit in time. But this does not mean that all can accept this with ease. When Arnold Palmer at nearly seventy went around his home course in Latrobe, Pennsylvania in sixty-three he couldn't stop himself from dreaming that somewhere inside him there was perhaps one more victory. Athletes give themselves in mind and spirit and body to competing and winning. It is what constitutes their identity. It is intense, all-engrossing, elemental, and when it goes it must leave a painful vacancy. 'I am happiest when I am in the hunt for the title,' Ballesteros has said. 'I am like the gambler. The great moment is not when the roulette wheel has finished spinning, and the gambler knows if he has won or lost. The great moment comes while the wheel is spinning, and he does not yet know the outcome. That's what I live for.' Older champions have been accustomed for so long to turning their minds towards getting in the hunt that when winning is no longer possible there is a loss of meaning. 'I can live without playing the Masters,' Jack Nicklaus has said. 'But the really satisfying time is the three weeks leading up to the Masters when I'm preparing for it.'

The tour can become a way of life, competing addictive. Many professional golfers, like boxers, go on when they can no longer compete as equals. But the time finally comes for all of them when it is over, when everything associated with tournament golf is behind them. Some may find a way of enjoying this, others not. 'Don't ever get old,' said Ben Hogan in 1971 when he withdrew from a tournament after eleven holes due to fatigue and pain. He'd hit three balls into a ravine on the par-three fourth, hurt his knee trying to hack the last of them out, and made a nine on the hole. He went out in forty-four and double-bogeyed ten and eleven.

When Chick Evans was well into his eighties my father received a Christmas card from him which included one of his lyrics.

My memory pauses for pleasing
retrospection of all the marvelous
dreams, remembering the best and
forgiving the rest.

The Masterpieces, long have I worked
back through the past on them; now
the world seems deaf because no one
listens; I feel pained at times.

We all face something that others
cannot know; all Earth's peoples share
the wait for Death to bring the slow
answers; Life's night comes when hope
is dead; 'til then grows the doubt that
never dies.

Perhaps this is old age for most people, or perhaps
this particular combination of pain and doubt and
isolation happens during an old age carrying with
it the memory of great deeds long past and mostly
forgotten, at least by others.

Thinking of this process, this journey through
time made by the champion golfer – the long wait,
the great labour, the display of imagination and
nerve and will, the isolation, the exposure of self –
the player that comes most frequently into my
mind is Ben Hogan. It is not that he was the best.
I think the question of who was the best is without
meaning. Nor is it that he was prototypical, for no
one was at all like him. It is that, with his silence,
his search for perfection and his ferocious deter-
mination, he was the most elementally expressive
of golf as a technique and golf as competition. It is
that he was somehow near the square root of all
that goes into defining these things. I never saw
him play at his best, or even saw him interviewed.
I vaguely remember watching on television when
he was in contention after the third round of the

1967 Masters, but he was fifty-five then and he faded before the final nine. What I know of him comes only from quotation and anecdote. But from this he seems the most mysterious of golfers, his life utterly covert and his golf a spectacle of naked will. He was driven by a search for perfection and, according to Dave Marr, got closer to it 'than any man who ever played the game'. Nicklaus, among others, thought him the finest striker of the ball he'd ever seen. A journalist watching him practise four-wood shots reported that the caddy 230 yards out in the field never had to take more than five paces to the right or left to collect the balls. He often went through 36-hole final days on fiercely difficult courses in major championships never missing a fairway or a green, and never speaking. He thought that on average he hit only one perfectly pure shot per round and that if he could average three or four he might shoot in the fifties. He once had a dream in which he made seventeen holes-in-one and a two. 'When I woke up,' he said, 'I was so God-damned mad.'

What drove him? When asked he said that he wanted to make enough money so as not to be a burden to his widowed mother. But could it also have been anger at the world, some need for vengeance? Some writers write, perhaps, and painters paint for this primeval reason. Céline, Knut Hamsun, Goya. Bob Dylan reached heights of eloquence driven by venom. What part of Shakespeare was Hamlet? Hogan had ample enough cause to be angry at the world. 'I had a tough day all my life,' he said. He grew up poor. He was in the room when his father killed himself with a .38 revolver shot to the head. He was small and was beaten around the caddy yard in Fort Worth, Texas until finally he beat up somebody bigger than him. He worked daemonically on his game but it was a long time before he won anything. Year after year he went out on the tour and came back broke. This frustrated him terribly. For a while during the winter tour in California he and his wife survived mainly on oranges they picked from the trees, and when they were down to their last eight dollars he came out of his motel room to find his car up on blocks and all the wheels stolen. He stood beating his fist into the wall. When finally he began to win major championships and dominate the tour his car was hit head-on by a bus on a narrow bridge on a foggy morning and his leg was smashed. Obituaries were read out on the radio, but he pulled through it. He went back out on the tour a year later and continued winning, but with a severely restricted schedule because of poor circulation in his leg. In 1953 he entered six tournaments and won five, three of them majors, including a win at the British Open at Carnoustie that remains legendary in Scotland. He might have made the Grand Slam had he entered the US PGA.

On the course he was intense, austere, laconic, enveloped inviolably in concentration. There was no humour or evident joy in his golf. Frivolity appalled him. He told his friend Claude Harmon that he had a good chance to win the US Open at Winged Foot because he was a good player and also the resident pro and therefore knew the course better than anyone, but that he wouldn't do it because he played what Hogan called 'jolly golf' – which for him was golf with conversation. He barely noticed a hole-in-one Harmon made when they were playing together at the Masters. George Fazio knocked in an eight iron for an eagle in front of his hometown crowd when playing with Hogan, and though the gallery went wild and play was delayed Hogan had no memory of it after the round. He hadn't a concept of a relaxing day on the course. 'I play golf with friends but we don't play friendly golf,' he said. When invited to play a round with the King of Belgium he said, 'I don't play golf while on holiday.' Golf was war, with the course, with the competition and with himself, and he had to win. You prepared for this war with long and punishing labour, and from this there was no escaping. When a young pro asked him for advice he said, 'Go dig it out of the ground like I did.' Bad shots made him want to vomit. In particular he loathed the hook, which plagued him in his early years. 'It's like a rattlesnake in your pocket,' he said. Hogan passed through many people's lives in his long career. He astounded spectators and players with his power and precision, his self-containment and ferocity. But it seems he remained unknown.

Hogan was, with Vardon, Jones, Hagen, Palmer and Nicklaus, an epoch-maker in the history of golf. They all moved the game on in some way. As nearly everyone who has even heard of golf knows, we are now in the era of Tiger Woods. He has moved the game on in the revenue he generates, the global spread of his fame, the quality and intensiveness of both his physical conditioning and the coaching he receives, the thoroughness of his preparation and the quality of his play. His game is fearsomely complete. He is enormously long. The golf journalist David Davies has calculated that a course would need to be 8,750 yards long in order for it to be a legitimate par seventy-two for him. He has a full array of shots with woods and irons, he appears to have the idea that anything from 120 yards in is makeable and that putts of twelve feet or less should all be holed. In all the time I have been watching golf I have never seen anyone make as many vital five- to twelve-foot putts as he does. His work around the green is miraculous. He is a vibrantly hungry competitor, his concentration is formidable, he appears to pace himself with intelli-gence over a round, a tournament and a season, and he appears also to have taken preparation for major championships to a new level. Before he went to St Andrews for the millennial British Open he watched videos of the course in a variety of weather conditions and pin placements so that he could know all the bounces and rolls, bring all the nuances of the course into his memory and make a plan, with contingencies, of how he wanted each shot to work. When his game is really on it seems to have some quality of the supernatural about it. I remember watching his third round at Augusta in 1997 and thinking I'd never seen golf played like that. He overwhelmed a course that has left many maimed, playing powerful, attacking, fearless golf. He hit a shot of astonishing self-confidence at the eleventh, directly at the flag, which had water immediately behind it. If he was just a few feet long he'd have been in the pond. He left it nearly dead and made the birdie putt.

There are those with a limited knowledge of the game who think it boring when he wins. They perhaps do not realize how difficult the game is, how seldom are his victories or how fragile any player's grasp of the game can be, even the best. I love to see him win. Like Palmer and Ballesteros, he plays an exuberant, thrilling and explosive version of the game and I think it a great fortune to be able to see it for, as Ernie Els has said, probably no one has ever played like that. There is an optimism about him. He ignites people's imaginations and spirits. They feel a familiarity with him, so that for the galleries he is Tiger as Palmer was Arnie or Ballesteros Seve, while Hogan, for example, remained Hogan.

After Tiger won at Augusta in 1997 Nicklaus declared that he could win more Masters titles than he and Palmer put together. Certainly if he plays as he is playing for long enough and no other similarly blessed individual appears to impede him he will break records believed to be unbreakable. What can stand in his way? Several things are possible. He swings very hard at the ball and with a violently fast hip action, so that it would seem to someone as unknowledgeable as myself that there is very little margin for error in the timing. He hits some very wild shots sometimes. I also wonder if he can carry such an uneaseful swing into his late thirties and forties. And his putting could go, like anybody's.

But I think that the threat to his reaching the fullness of his potential over the next twenty years is more likely to come, if it comes at all, from within him, from a diminution of hunger. Corporate advertisers could do it. They are already crawling all over him looking for ways to exploit his talent, his looks, his intensity, his blackness. They specialize in the appropriation of the engaging and substantial and individualistic. Iggy Pop, John

Lennon, Pablo Picasso and Labi Siffre have been used to sell cars. Photographs of political protest have been used to sell package holidays. Smirnoff even tried to use the famous iconographic portrait of Che Guevara to sell its vodka, but happily could not obtain the rights. The cynicism of the advertising world now runs so deep that it appears they are more interested in draining things of their meaning, of turning authenticity and passion into irony and chic, than they are even in selling their products. It could sicken the person thus used. It is profitable, but violating. Certainly Tiger Woods is as commercially exploitable as anyone now living and he would be wise to be cautious, as I imagine he is. His hunger to win could also be threatened by satiation, a wish for privacy and freedom of movement, or concentration on a family or a woman. Perhaps some of this affected him during his second year on the tour, a mediocre time by his standards during which he often, I thought, looked sullen. It is said that Michael Jordan advised him to leave the business to others and love the game as he'd loved it before.

I think ultimately his strength is that he is driven not only by a hunger to win, but also by a sense of destiny. He knows that it is a long story, and he wants to see it through to the end. He wants to leave a mark in time. He is, as C. L. R. James said of Sobers, 'expressing a personal vision'.

VI

Marooned with Brigitte Bardot

WHEN MY FRIEND RANG FROM *ESQUIRE* MAGAZINE to ask me what golf story I might like to write I told him that I would like to play a round with Arnold Palmer. He said that sounded fine and so I wrote a letter stating my case to 'Arnold Palmer, Latrobe, Pennsylvania', but it couldn't be arranged at that time and I wrote about other things. However, fifteen months later and just before New Year, 1993, I got word from Pennsylvania that if I still wanted to play golf with Mr Palmer I was to be at the first tee of the Bay Hill Club in Orlando, Florida at 12.20 p.m. on 12 January.

I arrived three days early with a bad back and nearly nauseous with nerves. There had been a time when he was the second person in golf for me after my father. I followed him around during his practice rounds when he came to Chicago for the Western Open and watched his progress on the tour, perpetually, it seemed, on the edge of my seat. The idea then of actually playing golf with him was the sort of idle notion boys entertain themselves with before going to sleep. Like punching out the local thug. Or being marooned somewhere with Brigitte Bardot. Now I was at Bay Hill and it was about to happen. His name and face were everywhere there because he is the club's owner. Palmer winning the Masters. Palmer and Jack Nicklaus. Palmer and a few Presidents. I stayed in the club's hotel and never left the grounds the entire time I was there, playing two practice rounds, putting, staying out on the range until it was dark. I saw him once at breakfast at a big table with friends and then later on his own prowling around a putting green at the back of the range like a bear in a cage. I didn't approach him. 'What's it like to play with him?' I asked Jim Deaton, the head pro. 'The first time I played with Mr Palmer,' he said, 'I couldn't feel my thumbs for the first eleven holes. I hardly said anything at all because I kept rehearsing everything in my mind before I said it so I'd get it right.'

The night before the round I lay on the floor in my room doing exercises for my back. I heard an irregular series of faint clicks outside, and I went onto the balcony to have a look. It was around midnight. The day had been cloudy, but a huge V-shaped fissure had opened in the sky to reveal a full moon and a knee-high white mist clinging to the bases of the palm trees and drifting along the ground. On the practice green below me four teenaged boys were having a putting contest. They looked incorporeal in the moonlight and mist. Just beyond them was the first tee. What was to happen to me there the next day at 12.20? Would I move the ball sideways three yards back between my legs? Would the driver fly out of my hands on the backswing? The father of a friend of mine was once invited to an outing at a club he had never played at before and, on the first tee, before a large crowd of waiting golfers, had swung and missed twice. On his third attempt the ball dribbled forward twenty yards to the ladies' tee. He then turned to his gallery, solemnly shook his head and said, 'Tough course.' At least I would have a line in the event of disaster.

The next morning I went out early and played five holes very badly. 'Please not today,' I whispered after each ballooned, blocked and topped shot. I ran back to my room to change my shirt and then over to the practice range. I got a few degrees of coordination back and then heard the starter announce through a loudspeaker, 'First group of the shoot-out to the tee please – Mr Palmer, Mr Damron, Mr Mitchell, Mr Dorman and Mr O'Grady.' Arnold Palmer came down the steps from the pro shop, put on a straw hat and walked over to the first tee. So did players coming off the ninth and eighteenth greens, everyone from the practice putting green, several from the driving range and swimming pool, caddies, waiters, club attendants, assistant pros and a number of people in the middle of their lunches. I did not turn around to see how many there were but from the way the skin was crawling on my back it felt like a multitude.

All four of my playing partners hit good, long drives into the heart of the fairway. Palmer's ball took off from the face of his large, metal-headed driver as if out of the mouth of a cannon and sailed into the atmosphere out of the range of my sight. I heard applause and a few whoops. I was last. My chest felt like it was in flames. Golf bags, tee markers and the trees up the fairway all looked out of proportion and shimmering, as if in a malign dream. I bent over to tee the ball up, looked along the ground and there, just a few feet away, was Arnold Palmer. I could see his white Nike shoes, his sharply creased trousers, the powerful veined forearms and blacksmith's hands, the fingers round and surprisingly short, like chipolatas. How had I come to be in this position? My hands were shaking so badly that the ball clattered on the tee like teeth in a cold wind. Above me, as if from the clouds, I heard him speak. 'Take it easy,' he said very softly. 'We're just here for an afternoon of golf. Enjoy yourself.'

I stood up, looked, I suppose, imploringly at the ball, and tried to stay intact as I took my swing. The ball came off the clubface a little to the inside of centre, climbed over a tree that guarded the slight dogleg and settled down on the left side of the fairway, seventeen yards behind Arnold Palmer's. Never had I struck a golf shot invested with such turmoil.

I watched his back as he strode down the fairway. Winner of seven major titles over a period of six years. At sixty-three the fourth highest money-earner in all of sport. Possibly the most widely admired and trusted man in America. He would play that day in a way that reminded me of the games I had played with fellow caddies as a teenager – free and easy, laughing a lot, going full-out for everything, a little angry at himself sometimes but also visibly loving the feeling of the ball being struck by the club. He still flailed at it with a violent, corkscrewing lunge. His drives carried 275 yards and I don't recall him missing a fairway with any of them. On a par three where I was using a three iron I noticed that he had hit a six.

Our fiveball team was one of around eight competing against each other that day, with each player throwing thirty dollars into a pot for the winning team and the best three scores on each hole counting. By the time we came to the sixteenth, a par five, we were three over as a team and out of the hunt. Arnold hit a two-iron second over the water into some thick grass on the front fringe of the green. When he half-fluffed the chip he winced as though someone had prodded him in the ribs and then said to the sky, 'If I knew how to play that shot I'd have won four more US Opens.' It occurred to me that I would be unlikely to hear that again on a golf course.

Just two holes left then. I could already feel the round slipping away like a passing dream and I longed to hold on to it. I had played with a moderate solidity and was eight over through sixteen, but then cracked up on the next, a long par three on which I hit two balls into the water and finished with a six. They were really hideous shots. I got a little round of applause from Arnold on the next, however, when I hit a four wood out of the rough and over water which landed next to the pin and stopped on the fringe of the green. He hit an eight iron for his second and finished one over for the day. I got a par for an eighty-three.

We headed for the clubhouse. Scott Hoch sped by on his own in a buggy. Arnold stopped to talk for a while with two teenagers and then went inside. We sat at a round table in the men's locker room and had three rounds of beers. I was so elated I felt I could have drunk vats of it. Andy Bean came in wearing long white socks and pressed Bermuda shorts. He was carrying two framed photographs he wanted Arnold to sign for some friends. Arnold smiled, said, 'Sure,' and as he wrote his name said to Bean, 'You're not playing golf in shorts are you?' Bean is a large, evidently relaxed and amiable man who won eleven times on the US Tour and played twice in the Ryder Cup, but in this moment he looked like a truant caught on his way out of a sweet shop. 'Well . . . ahhh . . . just, you know, trying to get some sun on the legs . . . very white the legs, after the winter . . .' he said, and then drifted away. Arnold waved and wished him well. He is gracious, easy and attentive in company, but also has a formidable natural authority. I would not like to cross him. Peter Alliss interviewed him at Augusta, having decided to attack him for taking a place there without having a chance to win. Arnold answered the charge patiently, explaining about the tradition at the Masters and the gallery's sense of it. But Alliss wouldn't let it go, asking him if it didn't embarrass him to play so poorly at such a great championship, to be an old man taking the place of a younger, more deserving player. 'Well it could be worse,' said Arnold. 'At least I'm not running around after people trying to interview them.'

We talked about a lot of things through the late afternoon – Hogan, Snead, his victory in the US Amateur – 'the one I am most proud of, I think' –

the sixty-five he shot while still in college at the Azalea Open, the fears that beset champion athletes and his rivalry with Jack Nicklaus – 'still as fierce as ever'. He was intelligent, unrestrained and interesting about these and other matters, but the subject that seemed to stir him most was his father. Years after his father's death and decades after he himself had become heroic to so many people, he was still clearly awed by him, a tough, compact steelworker and club pro from western Pennsylvania with a foreshortened foot. 'My father was one of the strongest men I ever met,' he said. 'He could do ten pull-ups with either arm and go practically all day if he used both. He was a severe disciplinarian and a great man for manners, but above all he had respect for other people. He told me that if I wanted to go to sleep with a clear conscience I should treat everyone I came across as if I myself were that person. It's a simple enough principle, but maybe it could be forgotten if you were tired or had a bad round. But he'd driven very deeply into me the idea that everyone has their story and that you must take them as they come and care about them. Anything else is undeserving of respect. Because of the way he raised me I don't think there was much chance of me going off the rails or acting like a big shot, but if I had, I know he would have been there to make me see sense. He was tough. For a long time I didn't think he believed I could play golf. I had won the US Amateur, several pro tournaments and two Masters before he even congratulated me. It was after the US Open at Cherry Hills and he said, "Nice going, boy." I thought the world had come to an end.'

We went out onto the grass to have some pictures taken for the article I was to write. The photographer placed us nose to nose, as if to suggest two boxers promoting a fight. We had to hold this pose for a long time. 'This would be a lot easier if you were a pretty girl,' said Arnold as he looked into my eyes. He wrote a note to my father, then small and enfeebled in his bed in Chicago. His wife called him then on his mobile phone and he told me he had to go. I watched him walk into the gathering darkness, hands in his pockets, checking the condition of his trees, whistling lightly, I thought, as he rounded a corner, a driven, successful yet unpretentious man. That was it then, my most memorable day on a golf course.

I went back to London and sent my father the note. He was about to become eighty-eight years old. He'd had a triple-bypass operation ten years earlier and finally retired from dentistry. The surgery invigorated him so much that in his first year of retirement he played up to three rounds of golf per week. When he was seventy-nine he was four over par after fifteen holes on the Navy airbase course where he was a member and needed to finish three over for the difficult final three holes in order to shoot his age. He went bogey, bogey, double bogey for eighty. Then, the following year, he began, it seemed, slowly to evaporate. His hands and face became skeletal. Sometimes he looked both haunted and bewildered, as though he feared something bad might be coming to him but could not understand why this should be. He had the same physical expectations he'd had more than thirty years earlier, but the body would not react as it had. 'Getting old,' he said, 'is without compensations.' He walked a few times per week to the school playing fields to hit nine irons from the same spot I had used as a teenager, but he ceased going to the golf course. I tried several times to get him to come with me when I visited him, but he wouldn't shift. 'If I swung a golf club now I'd fall over,' he said.

Finally, when he was eighty-six, I persuaded him to come out as a spectator for a round I was to play with three friends of his. He stayed sitting in his buggy with his eyes shaded by the brim of his hat until the twelfth hole, a par three, when he asked if he could hit a shot. He hadn't struck a golf ball in at least three years. The emaciation had now advanced so far that his flesh seemed like a fine layer of gauze over his bones. He looked terribly frail as he stood alone on the tee lining up the shot. I yearned for him to at least get the ball airborne. He took no practice swing. The club came back with a familiar little hitch near the top of the backswing, then the right knee kicked in and the right elbow stayed tight to the ribs as he accelerated smoothly and classically, the head down and behind the ball as he hit into and through the shot – all those elements of controlled abandon he had instructed me in decades before. It was as though there was an inner ghost moving the derelict frame. He hit it thin, but it ran up to the edge of the green.

VII

Mr O'Grady

ALL THROUGH MY LIFE I'D PLAYED GOLF ON courses I'd travelled to by public transport and where I'd changed shoes on a bench. I experienced a different, more rarefied form of the game when I began to write about it. I wrote several travel articles for *Golf World* and was now flying first- or business-class to other continents to play on championship courses designed by superstars and groomed, it seemed, with scissors. I'd stay in $500-per-night rooms in resorts which promoted themselves with laminated brochures decorated with photographs of rolling fairways in dawn light, soft-focus dining rooms, slender, elegant women in white gowns administering massages, and with phrases such as 'To be a success you need a little pampering sometimes'. I had the idea that I shouldn't be complicitous in this, but I wanted to see those countries and play those courses and would be unlikely to do so if I had to finance it myself.

I went to Thailand and to Kenya, where I played with my caddy and where the trees were full of monkeys. I went to Palm Springs, an abstract, rather provisional playground in the desert where the golf courses are made of blue lakes and vibrantly green fairways sculpted from a harsh wilderness where rattlesnakes once slithered in the grey dust. Water is so scarce that plants have learned to secrete a substance that kills any other vegetation attempting to grow near them. I played Mission Hills there, jackrabbits with ears the size of unhusked corn standing at the edges of the fairways. I also played the grand, sometimes sadistic PGA West Stadium Course, where Lee Trevino won $175,000 with a hole-in-one during a skins game on the island-green par-three seventeenth. I travelled along the north coast of Ireland and played the brutal Royal Portrush, which made me understand a little of how truly gruelling must be the four days of the British Open, and Royal County Down, which with its rolls and colours and vistas seemed to have been painted on the land. I played nine holes at Mediterraneo in Castillon with the ebullient Sergio Garcia in the summer before he turned pro, when his handicap was plus six – a world record, he had been told. In 1995 I played Oak Hill in Rochester, New York for a piece on that year's Ryder Cup. I played with the club president, who took me to a spot in the trees on the nearly 600-yard-long thirteenth to describe a shot struck by Severiano Ballesteros during a US Open. He had driven about forty yards into these woods on the left, with a ten-yard-wide, perhaps ten-foot-high corridor leading out between the trees to the fairway. This corridor was at an angle of around 135 degrees to the direction of the hole. Nearly anyone else would have simply punched the ball back onto the fairway, but Ballesteros took out a three wood, hit it low off the dirt and the leaves through the gap, and when the ball got out into the open it rose high into the air and took the 135-degree left turn to finish around 260 yards up the hole in the centre of the fairway. It was the most astonishing thing, said the president, that he'd ever seen on a golf course.

I went on an extravagantly luxurious trip to Hawaii with a group of journalists which included Lord Bill Deedes. I imagined not taking well to a Tory peer and friend of the Thatchers, but he was fine and very amusing company, with views which surprised me about Africa, the IMF and Ireland. I asked him who was the best speaker he'd ever heard. 'Lloyd George,' he said. He might have said Disraeli or Pitt the Younger, so much a figure of antiquity did Lloyd George seem to me. We played Mauna Lani, site of several Seniors' skins games, and a great cliffside Nicklaus course on Lanai'i.

I played a few times that week with a four-handicapper named Steve Carr.

'Have you ever dreamed about golf?' he asked me as we were walking along after our balls.

'Yes I have,' I said. 'Quite often.'

'I can tell you what you dreamed,' he said.

'Go on,' I said.

'You are on the first tee waiting to hit your drive. The course is open and inviting and you can't wait to hit your first shot, but when you get up on the tee, walls and doors start appearing so that you can't take a backswing, or there is a tiny door set at an extreme angle to the fairway which you have to hit the ball through. More and more things appear to thwart you, the ball dropping off the tee, the club breaking apart in your hands. The dream fades away as you keep trying to hit your drive and with new obstacles appearing to stop you.'

He was right. This was one of the archetypes of my dream life, like the unprepared-for exam. John Updike has written a short essay about this affliction, in which golf balls can suddenly become cylindrical – 'a roll of coins in a paper wrapper, or a plastic bottle of pills' – and the swing is made 'in a straitjacket, through masses of cobwebs'. Yet 'the dreamer,' he reports, 'surrenders not a particle of hope of making the shot.' I had a dream just before beginning this book in which I was waiting on the first tee behind a twoball playing a nine-hundred-and-something-hole match, followed by a Moonie who was accompanied by Serbs in athletics costumes doing sprints on the fairway. I was to play a match with an old friend of mine from Chicago whom I badly wanted to beat, but when our turn came and I took out my driver I found it was missing the central inset piece on the face. I went running into a vast basement with many doors, looking for another driver, the dream ending as I ran deeper and deeper into this darkening labyrinth, the route back to the golf course growing more obscure but with my need to strike a shot becoming yet more urgent.

The most spectacular of all these trips was to western Canada, where I travelled in a large group from Kananaskis, near Calgary, to Banff, then up past blue-white glaciers and ice fields to Jasper Park, where Doug Wood hooked his chip shot, and finally across the Rockies by train all the way to Vancouver and then north to Chateau Whistler, where you can ski in the morning and play golf in the afternoon. These are four world-class courses which have a thematic coherence not only because of their mountain settings but also because of their architects. The two oldest, Banff and Jasper, were designed by Stanley Thompson. Robert Trent Jones Senior, the designer of Kananaskis, was apprenticed to Thompson and eventually became his business partner. He was also the father of Robert Trent Jones Junior, the designer of Chateau Whistler.

My favourite was Banff. It is set a mile high in a mountain wilderness with two rivers running through it, built on topsoil which was hauled up by rail and mule. Thompson designed it by entering the woods with a bottle of gin and sitting down at the base of the pines until he could feel the holes forming in his mind. There are jokes, deceptions, surprises and overwhelming vistas. Fairways are contoured to follow the shapes of the mountain ranges above them, but sometimes the tees are skewed a little to dupe you into taking the wrong line. Bunkers that you think are tight to the green flare up forty-five yards short. These and the mountains destabilize your sense of distance so thoroughly that you can be four or five clubs out, as Gene Sarazen once was, unless you go strictly by the yardage. There is a hole there where you climb a quarter of a mile upwards to the old professionals' tee and drive over a river that has come crashing down through waterfalls and rapids and that throws up spray below you like fistfuls of diamonds, the ball falling in a long arc hundreds of feet down onto a bending fairway cut through a forest of pine.

When Thompson had designed the course and laid much of it out he found a narrow deep bowl in the landscape with a glacial pond at its base, its surface weirdly mottled from the massive rocks on the pond bed. He rearranged his plans and built a new hole there. It is one of the most memorable and mysterious holes I have ever played, a par three with a carry of 160 yards from the side of a mountain down through eerie blue-green light to the green, the still water reflecting the pine trees, the rockface and the sky.

I was in a group which was first out that day. It was bright and warm, the air brilliantly clear, the company genial and entertaining, eagles and hawks soaring above and great bull elks strolling along the fairways with their harems, sharpening their racks of antlers for the bloody wars of the mating season soon to come. They make a sound described as 'bugling', a strange mixture of the plaintive and the fierce. If I was assigned to play only Banff for the rest of my life I believe I would never tire of it.

What makes a great golf course? For most of my golfing life I'd never faced the question because I'd never played on one. But since I began writing about golf I'd played on courses designed by Pete Dye, Donald Ross, Alister Mackenzie, Stanley Thompson, Jack Nicklaus, the Fazios, Trent Jones Senior and Junior, H. L. Colt and Old Tom Morris. Golf courses have been laid out over lava beds and desert floor, along cliffsides and in orchards, through rainforest, mountains, woodland and of course through seaside duneland once used for sheep grazing. They can have the feel of amphitheatres, sculpture parks, high dives and boxing rings. There can be no objective criteria for comparing them. The making of a great golf course is like the creation of a work of fiction. It is an imagined order imposed on, and sometimes against, what is offered by nature. This is true even of links, the most natural of courses. You can see it from the air – the green strips and even greener targets slinking through the pale dunes, the round grey bunkers scattered like coins dropped from a leaking pocket. At the other extreme is desert golf, with its vast lakes and imported topsoil, the falls and rolls of the land made by earth-moving equipment from an architect's drawing. But to try to judge Pinehurst, for example, as better or worse than Troon is, I think, no more fruitful than attempting the same with Faulkner and Evelyn Waugh.

But as with fiction there are golf courses which are lazy, dull, cheap, tricky, and there are courses which are undeniably magnificent. A great golf course will have in some commonly held sense a beautiful setting and will suggest, even if through contrivance, the delicacy and power of nature. It will not reek of corporate capitalization, as in courses set down in real estate developments. It must be kept with an evident care and attention to detail and be of sufficient length to bring into play the full range of clubs. An architect and the greenskeeper who maintains what has been designed will consider the framing, texture, colour and contour offered by the land so that each hole becomes a kind of painting. Each hole thereby has the feeling of being utterly in its own world. A good golf shot feels more splendid on a great hole. It is as though the hole has lent a portion of its grandeur to the shot.

A golf course involves a journey in which the traveller, at least at the beginning, is open, curious and willing to be engaged, and it should have as much variety as the setting and the architect's personal sensibility allow while retaining the overall unity of a single authorship. A great golf course will have some holes which are conundrums, some epics, and some short, intense lyrics, with perhaps an oasis on each nine. There is often humour on a great golf course – as in Thompson's flared bunkers at Banff, holes made out of unlikely terrain, a small, sly hazard placed just where a cynical or absent-minded shot might land. All along the way, as in an allegory, the architect is asking questions of the golfer. Most are fair and democratic enough to offer the possibility of a range of answers so that players of all levels of ability can remain engaged in the process, but you will always best be able to appreciate a great course from the back tees, for it is the professional with whom the architect is most fundamentally in dialogue.

Finally, in my opinion, a great golf course will not, or at least should not, have artificial waterfalls or fountains spewing up from its water hazards. You see more and more of these things now. They are distracting and trite. They are like a Spice Girls lyric inserted into *Astral Weeks*.

In December 1995 I was sent by *Golf World* to Cadiz in southern Spain to play San Roque and Valderrama and then north to play a few courses around Valencia. San Roque, where each year hopeful pros enter the *corrida* of the European Tour qualifying school, is a pretty and playable course, but it has a fountain in one of its water hazards. The great Valderrama, the number one course in continental Europe and site of the first Ryder Cup to be played outside the United States or Britain, is tough, fascinating, and kept virtually to what I imagine are Augusta standards, though flawed too, I think – the seventeenth and eighteenth, for example, and the little rockery and waterfall on the fourth. But none of these are as bad as its insufferable pretentiousness.

I flew on to Valencia. I had a letter with me from a public relations company in London which informed me that I was to be met at the airport by

Maria Ruiz of the Valencian tourist authority, who, the letter said, would be very pleased to have dinner with me that night. On the way I looked down at the beige and green mountains and occasionally wondered who Maria Ruiz was. I formed tentative pictures. At the airport I collected my golf clubs and suitcase and walked through the arrivals door. I saw then a lovely looking blonde woman in a grey short-skirted suit holding with some embarrassment a sign which said 'Mr O'Grady'. She drove me in her little car through rice fields to the hotel where I was to stay and we sat in a conservatory there deciding which courses I would play over the next three days, the sky suddenly turning purple and green, huge low black clouds churning and rolling, a hurricane-like wind blowing the rain like a prolonged drum tattoo against the glass and the sea smashing against the breaker walls. I couldn't take my eyes off her.

I played Trent Jones Senior's El Bosque, set in hills surrounded by orange groves, and then Bernhard Langer's impressive Panoramica in a snowstorm. I liked them both very much, but neither were in the same rarefied world as the magnificent El Saler, set down by Javier Arana in duneland near the rice fields and the Albufera Lake to the south of the city. This is a beautifully flowing, richly imaginative course full of diversity, intelligence, treachery and spectacular vistas. Each nine starts among pines and then finishes as a links, the wind, the colours and the translucence of the air changing as the course opens out. The greens are huge, which adds to the sense of grandeur. The fairways have a generous width, but anywhere off them contains either thick, club-snaring grass or the kind of sandy badland into which you can disappear and then emerge five shots later. At almost any point your round can suddenly unravel. I watched Darren Clarke take ten strokes on the par-five fifteenth during the last round of the 2001 Spanish Open there.

El Saler is authentic, inspired, beautiful, intriguing and without mediocrity at any point. Above all it is natural, the holes having been found in the rolls and folds of the sandy land. They have the feeling of surprise and inevit-ability T. S. Eliot said constituted great poetry. Desmond Muirhead said of Alister Mackenzie's Augusta National that it 'is like a woman with a superb bone structure. That was Mackenzie's strength – structure. There have been few archi-tects with sufficient ability to make great holes on the land as it stood rather than always reworking the land to make the holes. Mackenzie was one of them.' On the evidence of El Saler, Arana was another. Sometimes, as in art, there is an astonish-ing confluence of material and mind in which the architect surpasses himself and a masterpiece is produced. When Arana finished building El Saler it is said that he sat down on the first tee and wept, perhaps at its beauty, perhaps because he believed he would never again do so well. I admired it as much as any course I have ever played, including PGA West, Royal County Down and Banff.

Maria came with me to Panoramica and met me most days for lunch and for dinner. This, it seemed, was part of her job. On the last night I took her to dinner and beforehand we sat in a wonderful bar with beamed ceilings and the walls hung with dark portraits. She spoke of her father. 'In a room full of people I always know where he is. I have to know that he feels all right.' Lucky man, I thought, to be loved like that.

I went back to London. I'd been with Maria so regularly during those few days that it seemed odd to be without her. I found reasons to call her every now and again. We exchanged a few letters. I tried to find ways of seeing her that would not seem too overtly like pursuit, but she parried every attempt. Finally, seven months later, she called me to say she was going to the Scottish Open at Carnoustie for work purposes. 'Will you be there?' she said. I had never reported on a golf tournament in my life and there was no prospect of me reporting on this one. 'Yes,' I said.

She drove to Edinburgh and once again was

waiting for me at an airport. We went to a few bars and had dinner on a little terrace, watching white-faced mimes darting from portal to portal in some inscrutable act, and then drove to Dundee. We sat in my hotel bar until 5.00 a.m. waiting for the answer to the single, pervasive, all-defining question that had been hanging in the air ever since her phone call. The light came early into my room and we had a glorious day that had the feeling of revelation out in wild, heathery hill-land near Perth. She didn't work much at Carnoustie, but when she did I walked around the course watching the pros. I followed Montgomerie and Woosnam and some Swedes I'd never heard of. I saw from a distance Eamon Darcy's unmistakable whirligig swing on the eighteenth, where in 1999 Jean van de Velde later descended for a time through the concentric spheres of golfing anguish. The course looked impossible, I thought.

Maria and I met on working trips of hers to Prague and Paris. I joined her at the British Open at Troon, where Arnold Palmer won his sixth major and where a friend of mine from Derry lost his virginity. He was an apprentice electrician there and the event took place beside a bunker on the internationally renowned par-three eighth, known as the 'Postage Stamp'. We went to New York and to Cuba and soon I was living half the time in Valencia. I began to play at El Saler and eventually became a member. I play there now sometimes with a Basque doctor, Miguel Juantegui, who periodically through his life has discovered the secret of golf. It hits him suddenly, like Socrates' fits of abstraction. Once it came upon him while he was ascending alone in a lift in the hospital in Brussels where he was studying his speciality. He was there, hair groomed, tie straight, white coat, stethoscope. Something suddenly and dramatically entered his mind about the hip turn. He bent over and began vigorously swinging an imaginary club, making explosive sound effects of the club hitting the ball and it then sizzling like a firework through the air. What he did not realize until he looked up was that the lift door had opened and a crowd of people were watching him. He tried whistling and scratching his back as though this was all that he had been doing, but he thinks they weren't convinced.

By the summer of 1998, two and a half years after my brief golfing tour around Cadiz and Valencia, Maria and I were expecting the birth of our daughter Beatriz. A novel of mine called *I Could Read the Sky* had been published the previous year and I was moving myopically around the foothills of another. The work was slow and sometimes harsh. Two, sometimes three afternoons a week I'd go to El Saler and play golf. It was the only thing other than sleep which could silence the book for a while. I'd have some good stretches on the course, but it was very difficult for me to put together an entire round there. I longed to break eighty before Beatriz was born, for I knew that regular golf was soon to come to an end, as it had for my father after my birth.

I went out alone one hot July afternoon, with the wind coming from the inland plains, an unusual wind called the *poniente* which carries a brutal, dry, deoxygenated heat. At its worst the *poniente* can make you feel that your eyes are about to melt. There were very few around El Saler that day and I played alone. I stood on the first tee thinking as ever about bringing in a score under eighty and hit a drive out to the right that rolled off the fairway and stopped behind a tree. I knocked it back out onto the fairway and hit a weak, pushed, ugly eight-iron shot short and right of the green, leaving me with a pitch over a bunker that had to stay under the limbs of an overhanging tree. I skulled it over the green, made a mediocre pitch and two-putted for a triple-bogey seven. That's the round over, I thought, at the first station. I parred the next four, with birdie putts sliding just over the edge on three of them. I came to the sixth, the hardest hole on the course, I think – a 445-yard, treeless, wind-exposed par four that rolls through the sandy land to a very long green protected by a bunker on the right. You drive into a hill and if you don't hit it long enough the second shot is blind. The hole falls away along the left into a vicious rough of sand and shrubs, with more, similar oblivion to the right. The fairway is generous, but the wind reduces it greatly and the tee shot is nerve-wracking. I made a reasonable drive but then hit a low, misstruck three iron short left. I ran the next shot up to about eight feet and missed the putt for a par.

The front nine closes with two short, cunningly designed par fours with two-tiered greens and a short par three set down in a bowl in the sand. The eighth is inspired, a 330-yard par four running parallel to the beach and made into a dogleg by a sandy, flower-strewn wasteland left and with the approach complicated by a high dune right and a severely left-sloping green. When I began to play this course I thought these three holes among the easiest, but I now know how much precision is required for both the drives and approach shots on the two par fours. While for the professional, with his superior control, knowledge of a course is clearly an advantage, for a middling player it can tend to increase the panic because all the dangers are engraved on the mind. A par on the eighth, in particular, is a considerable relief to me. On this day I hit the seventh in regulation but three-putted from the bottom tier for a bogey, and then parred eight and nine. I'd shot a five-over-par forty-one.

I walked over to the tenth tee. I met there a retired professor of anthropology who spoke a rich and ornate Spanish, and I asked him if he'd like to join me. I hit a reasonable drive and we strode off together. I bogeyed the hole with a mediocre chip from the back fringe, but then birdied the next two, a long par five and a par three, with a pair of forty-foot putts. I was now four over after twelve and the round was taking on another complexion. On the thirteenth my birdie putt sat on the lip. Around this time I was addressing the ball incorrectly, with feet and hips square to the target, but with the shoulders open and the right arm stiff. I found this out a week later when I played with Dionisio Garcia, a former member of the Spanish national team, which at the time also included Jose Maria Olazabal. The consequence of this flaw on the fourteenth was a tee shot hit way out to the right, nearly to the adjacent fairway. I was left with a five-wood shot from a slightly tight lie over some low pines and a greenside bunker, and I got the ball to the right side of the green. It was the best shot I'd hit that day. The professor enthused in an agitated way about it. The birdie putt ran around the hole and sat on the back edge. I was four over with four to play. I could bogey three of them and still break eighty.

The back nine closes with a tree-lined, ever-narrowing par five, a middle-length, straight par four with out of bounds on the left, a beautiful 190-yard par three with dunes and bunkers all around and played straight at the sea, and finally a majestic 440-yard doglegging par four that rolls down to an enormous green, dunes and the sea to the right. The wind was rising. I was nervous as I faced these holes and found myself standing for a long time over each shot. I hit two solid woods down the fifteenth and was left with an eight or perhaps nine iron into the wind from the centre of the fairway. My mind was running around like a swarm of gnats. I took the eight and did what my father told me I must not do – I gave up on the shot, hitting it short and right into a bunker. I hit it out and two-putted for a six. I'd used the first of the three bogeys. I parred the next, with the long birdie putt again running up to the hole, rolling around it slowly and sitting on the edge. I hit a low, unintentional fade with a three iron to the seventeenth, an unappealing but effective enough shot that left me with a long putt down from the upper tier. I got a par with a five-foot second putt.

If I ended the round as I had begun it, with a triple bogey, I would not break eighty. This was certainly possible. The eighteenth has out of bounds on the left and the dunes on the right are covered with crawling seaside flowering plants that obscure golf balls and from which it is nearly impossible to extricate yourself. I hit the drive left of centre with a slight draw and the ball rolled down into a bunker. I was at the forward edge under a high lip. I thought first of a four iron and then of a seven. Had I used either of these clubs the ball would almost certainly have driven into the lip and rolled back into the sand. Unusually for me I made a sensible decision. I knocked a pitching wedge down the left side and then from light rough hit a six iron into the wind about ten feet to the right of the hole. The putt went in for a par and the professor of anthropology emeritus shook my hand, clapped me on the back and told me in his courtly manner that he was going to have a bottle of wine with his dinner that night and tell his wife all about the wonderful way I had played the back nine at El Saler. I was five over on the front nine and even on the back for a seventy-seven.

After the round I drove over to the Nueve de Octubre hospital where Maria had an appointment with her obstetrician.

'Do you know what happened today?' I said when I saw her.

'What?' she said. She was tired, hot and eight and a half months pregnant.

'I shot seventy-seven at El Saler. After a triple bogey on the first. Eight birdie putts missed by less than an inch!'

'What else happened today,' she said, 'is that I had the last of the ultrasound examinations before the birth of our baby. Do you want to know how it was?'

Bragging about golf is truly repulsive. It is like bragging about sex. No one wants to hear about it and the braggart acquires a malodorous aura which stays long in the memory of the recipient. I have had very little to brag about regarding golf, so it has been for the most part an easy matter to avoid this obnoxious practice. Yet despite these strictures and Maria's riposte in the hospital, I could not quite bring myself to stay quiet about my round at El Saler. I came home and telephoned a friend in London with whom for a year or so I had had a regular weekend game. I was a little like the matador who ran directly from bed into the bars in the street outside to tell everyone that he'd just made love with Ava Gardner. It did not seem like bragging, as I knew the round had nothing to do with mastery. As was perhaps the case with the matador, it was the uniqueness of the event that was the point. I knew that I would resume my irregular, pedestrian and sometimes loathsome style of playing, as indeed I did. 'I'm sorry,' I said to my friend on the other end of the line. 'I know this is tedious and probably even distasteful . . .' He listened with as much indulgence and grace as I could have asked for.

I am now, I suppose, not significantly better or worse at golf than I was when I was eighteen. I could fade the ball more consistently then and was better out of sand because I was hitting hundreds of shots from the bunker beside the green that was in front of the starter's office. But I can sometimes draw the ball, as I could never deliberately do before. I've collected a few tips along the way, which I continue to use and to value, the best two of which are, first, from Jack Nicklaus, which is to slow down the backswing almost to the point of the ridiculous when out of rhythm – for, as Bobby Jones said, 'No one ever swung a golf club too slow' – and, second, from my father, which is to hit fast downhill putts, and particularly downhill breaking putts, off the toe of the putter in order to deaden the impact. This allows you to make an accelerating yet delicate stroke. I know more about the swing now, but I am also more fearful. Fear seems to accumulate with age – fear of not completing one's work, fear of losing someone, fear of out of bounds. I am longer, I think, but that is probably ball technology. I have learned little about putting and course management and next to nothing about chipping and other types of shots around the green. I still think too much about spectacular shots and making a good score instead of taking each shot as it comes in a calm way, and have not found a way to absorb or change the anxiety and frustration that go along with this. I cannot clear the mind, bring in nothingness and repose or sustain a sense of ease and simple pleasure on a golf course, unless, of course, everything is going splendidly. I still play rounds as I did then, with a dozen pars or so interspersed with double and triple bogeys. This, compounded by the game's very nature, keeps alive the lifelong illusion that if I apply myself I can somehow bring it all under control. This is the comedy and seductiveness of golf.

There have been times when I've felt a powerful inclination to try to do something about it, to try to push on to another level. In the early 1990s I told my father that I was thinking of taking lessons when I returned to London. 'No, no,' he said. 'That's not a good idea. You don't need technique. You've got a caddy's swing.' I said something similar to my friend Caryl Phillips. 'I want to get on top of this game,' I said. 'I'm going to put in some time.' His reaction was as emphatically negative as my father's, though his reasons were different. 'There's only room for one obsession,' he said. The golf shot, the sentence. One has certainly fascinated me, but the other has been a thing of identity and desire, and though I suppose I am not much closer to the purity of the sentence than I am to the purity of the golf shot, the pursuit of it has driven and shaped my life. I of course cannot say that about golf. So I do not dispute what my golfing and novel-writing friend said to me about the exclusivity of obsession. I am to remain, then, in a golfing purgatory of the middle ranks, dreaming of a single sub-par round that I could replay again and again in my mind the way that men often summon pictures of the women they have known, but ever watching, as in Loudon Wainwright's song,

> Balls drop in the sand trap.
> Balls drop into ponds.
> Balls drop into ponds.

VIII

Symposium

SOME TIME DURING MY EXILE FROM GOLF IN THE
1970s I went into a second-hand bookshop in
north London and found a copy of a book called
Golf in the Kingdom by Michael Murphy. It had
on its cover an inaccurately drawn pair of hands
poised at the top of a backswing. I had never heard
of the book before, though it is now one of the
classics of golf literature and is also the primary
text of a small cult. I read in the little author's
biography inside that Murphy was a founder of
the Esalen Institute at Big Sur on the California coast, a centre dedicated to the study of eso-
teric aspects of medicine, psychotherapy, Eastern
religion, physics and, subsequent to the fame of
the book, golf. I bought it, took it home.

In it are a number of short mystical meditations
on various aspects of the game, but the bulk of it is
composed of a wonderfully compelling fictional
narrative of a round of golf played by Murphy, a
tall, bearded teaching pro named Shivas Irons and

a pupil of Irons named MacIver at a Scottish links course named Burningbush. Under the otherworldly yet trenchant tutelage of Shivas Irons, Murphy's game disintegrates to the point where he can barely hit the ball, but it then magically reconstitutes itself before the end. It is the story of a journey down into the darkness and up again into the light, with breakdown and liberation between, and by the end Murphy sees with an acuity previously unknown to him. I have read a few golf books awkwardly infused with mysticism, but because of the vividness of Murphy's characters, his narrative skill, his wit and the evident depth of feeling, honesty and undeviating tenacity with which he tells the story, the mixture here seemed natural, entertaining and revelatory.

Later, long after the round is over, whisky flows at a gathering at the house of a friend. The guests dance wild reels around the floor and Murphy and Shivas Irons erupt into the dark night, head for the links and play a treacherous, windblown par three after midnight with a pair of featheries and a shillelagh. Shivas has a hole in one.

This has followed a dinner at which the guests have convened, as in Plato's *Symposium*, to discuss love, specifically their love of golf. Peter, the host, declares that he has a name for each of his numerous golfing personalities – 'Old Red', for example, and 'Palsy' and 'Divot'. Driven on by the

151

whisky, he stalks metaphor. Golf is an 'X-ray of the soul', he says, and a links one long Rorschach test. Finally, triumphantly, it is like marriage. Both require 'steadiness of purpose and imagination, long shots and delicate strokes, steady nerves and a certain wild streak. And ye've got to have it *all* goin' or the whole thing goes kaflooey.'

Julian, the town doctor and psychiatrist, believes that players should traverse the eighteen holes dancing a Highland fling to live bagpipe music. 'Golf is the yoga of the supermind,' says a tiny ecologist named Adam. They discuss hitting balls from mountaintop to mountaintop in Peru and how golf courses are exploded gardens.

'Men lovin' men, that's what golf is,' declares Agatha, wife of Peter.

As in the *Symposium*, the definitive statement is the final one. 'All art and love depend on fascination,' says Shivas Irons. 'Life is nothin' but a series of fascinations, an odyssey from world to world. And so with golf. An odyssey it is – from hole to hole, adventure after adventure, comic and tragic. The game requires us to join ourselves to the weather, to know the subtle energies that change each day on the links, and the subtle feelin's of those around us. It rewards us when we bring them all together. In all o' that 'tis a microcosm o' the world, a good stage for the drama of our self-discovery . . . The grace that comes from such a discipline, the extra feel in the hands, the extra strength and knowin', all those special powers ye've felt from time to time, begin to enter our lives . . . Devoted discipline and grace will bring ye knowin's and powers everywhere, in all your life, in all your works if they're good works, in all your loves if they're good loves. Ye'll come away from the links with a new hold on life, that is certain if ye play the game with all your heart.'

I wondered as I read this, and have wondered since, what I would have said had I been at that dinner. One single chance to make a panegyric about an abiding fascination. It seems a grave responsibility. Speaking, like golf, is a variable activity. The same person can be oafishly incoherent or nearly mute one night, the words turning to vapour as he reaches for them, and as mellifluous as Oscar Wilde the next. I suppose the whisky would have helped. And of course it is less difficult to speak about something you love, something which has ignited and continues to ignite something inside you. In such cases it can be more difficult to stop speaking than to speak well.

What is it about golf that ignited something within me? In a certain light the question seems absurd. It is a sport, to some only a hobby, and at that a ridiculous hobby. I once read a description of golf reducing it to an activity which 'allows fat, spoiled, middle-aged businessmen to dress up like pimps'. But for some reason I have felt towards golf that same quickened feeling of inner identification that I have felt towards certain books, and certain people. What are the elements of golf that do this to me? I don't entirely know. Excitement is not constructed. It happens too rapidly to be analysed. We know only that we are engaged, that the prospects of fascination appear to be endless, that we want to go on being engaged and fascinated and that we fear or are hostile towards anything or anyone that might prevent us from doing so.

I suppose I, like other golfers, react as I do to the sport because a round of golf is a journey and all journeys are stories and everyone loves stories. Even if made repeatedly over the same terrain the journey is never the same and the story is therefore always told as if for the first time. Each time, the player sets out with aspirations for a happy ending but with no idea if he will find it. It is full of engrossment, suspense, unpredictability. Along the way the player will need tact, nerve, preparation, patience, skill, imagination, strength and delicacy to deal with the challenges and illusions and demons and angels and sirens that he meets, hope and despair in constant interplay, with, perhaps, a rare moment of glory. All of these are in some ways aspects of himself. We face ourselves all around the golf course, with every

154

shot. The glory, or the dream of it, draws us back to the start of the journey again and again. The despair is hideous and abasing, a kind of conflagration that in the moment of its happening threatens to devour us. We feel we want to lobotomize ourselves with our five irons. It is also comic, if seen from a slight distance. From this there is something to learn.

The player never ceases in the learning of the game. He tries to learn many things, but above all he is trying to learn to align mind and body, so that in the moment of the shot the mind is all body and the body all mind and intention is finally one with action. It almost never happens. The mechanisms involved in this alignment are profoundly subtle and elusive and fragile. Failure repeatedly succeeds upon failure. Golf reveals the complexity and difficulty of this task more acutely than anything I know, yet perhaps because of the difficulty, as in revelation or in art, the feeling in those rare moments when everything comes together is wondrous, explosive. For this the striving goes on, the journey is set out upon again. It is a journey of which the player is the only author. Unlike almost all other sports, golf is neither reactive nor collaborative. The player instigates each action in his own time and when he has done it finds himself in a place where only he has put himself. It is existential, a game of solitary accountability in which there is nowhere to hide. This gives it a cleanness, a transparency, not present in most of the other things that we do.

I might have said these and perhaps other things as they occurred to me while I drank the whisky and looked at the other golf-deranged faces around me at the dinner. But if I were allowed time to speak about only one thing it would have been the exhilaration of flight. This is one of the most, perhaps for me the most, elemental pleasures of golf. It is all so improbable – the tiny ball, the tiny target so far away, the peculiar-looking instrument that launches the ball from a still position through human mechanical strength alone in some mystery of physics, so much further than any other struck object in sport, the shot cracking in the silent arena of the hole like the report from a rifle, the ball sailing over the terrain, high above the tallest trees and dunes, over mists or rivers or hill-land or the backs of whales, still climbing against a backdrop of sky or mountain or the rising or setting sun, the ball seeming to define the land and architecture beneath it, the player seeming to assume the sensation of its flight, until it begins its descent, the destination uncertain, nervously anticipated, the ball gathering speed as it falls and strikes the land finally just in the heart of the target. Or not, as the case may be. Everybody wants in some way to fly. Golf allows you to do it, through the eye and in the spirit.

When I met Tom Watson I asked him if he'd ever read *Golf in the Kingdom*.

'I have,' he said. 'And I admired it.'

'Do you remember the scene after the round of golf when they go to a house and have dinner and talk about how much they love golf?'

'I do,' he said.

'If you were there,' I said, 'what would you have said?'

'The history of golf has been filled with so many fine men,' he said. 'There's a great dignity and sense of decency in the game. When you look at other areas of human activity, certainly the quality of the people who have excelled at golf says much, by comparison, about the quality of the game. In all the other American sports – basketball, baseball, football – players are always trying to find ways around the rules. They are even applauded for it. But in golf if you break the rules you are seen to be less of a person. Honesty is fundamental to it. It is a game of personal reckoning. You have to accept the rules even if you don't like them, you have to absorb your mistakes, learn to contend with anger and doubt, and play without complaint or special pleading. You cannot persuade yourself that you have hit a good shot when you have hit a bad one. These are things which when applied to living make you a better person. I think in this way golf can enhance a person, or even transform him.'

Sometimes after a round of golf or in bars late at night I'd ask friends of mine the same question. Nothing remains in my mind of their answers. Perhaps it is my poor memory or the lateness of the hour or that they hadn't anything ready. It is also true that most people don't have an analytical consciousness travelling along ghostlike in parallel with everything they do. I'd sometimes wondered how my father would have fashioned a statement, though I'd forgotten to ask him whenever I went to visit him. Why do you love it so much? What in you does it express? These were the questions that had remained unasked.

I had three chances to ask them in 1993, the last of them in October when I stopped in Chicago on my way back to London from playing golf in western Canada. It had been by then more than three years since my mother died. He had begun his long, slow decline long before that, but subsequently, on each of the anniversaries of her death, he had suffered increasingly debilitating crises that had hospitalized him and left him still more frail than before. Throughout those years I was in London hearing news about his health from himself or his doctors or his friends and had to gamble on when was the best time to travel to see him. I had to hope I would not be too late.

In that year I had visited him in May and then again in August. He'd survived up to then living alone with a woman coming in a few afternoons a week to cook for him. That summer he told me he could no longer go on like that. He hadn't the strength. He was too nervous. I found someone willing to live with him full-time, an intelligent and dignified Filipino woman who in her youth had wanted to become a nurse but had been prevented by her parents from doing so. She seemed to know when to leave him alone and when to give him company. Sometimes in the evenings she brought a small electric piano into his room and sang for him.

I found him in bed in his pyjamas when I arrived from Canada, utterly skeletal, his diminished head like a small piece of fruit on the pillow. He no longer dressed for the day and rarely got out of bed. Eating had become a misery. I came and went from his room through the week, talking with him and sometimes playing music for him on a little tape machine. Once I came in to find him standing up with his pyjamas around his ankles and a visiting nurse crouched at his feet bathing him. He looked at me as if to say, What do you think of this? He told stories and listened intently and laughed as before, but it was all paler now, and fading. I told him about interviewing Tom Watson at Sandwich that summer and about Watson's team winning the Ryder Cup at the Belfry just the week before. I also told him about my extraordinary time in Canada and about the great courses I'd played there, particularly Banff, which I described in operatic language. Perhaps I was excessive. He listened, his eyes widening as I spoke, and then said with some alarm, 'You speak as though this was the most amazing experience of your life.' He was right. I hadn't the measure of the experience, or of his capacity to hear about it or of how to look at him in the condition he was in.

On the day that I left I looked into his eyes and saw that they were already half in another world. He'd given up the struggle and didn't seem to mind. The eyes were dreamy and serene. He'd lived straight, so far as I knew. He was square with everyone of importance to him. He had no strength left and there was no point looking for more, for it wouldn't come. Letty, the Filipino woman, was allowing him to die by removing the need to struggle. What could I do to hold him a little longer in the world? My suitcase was at the door, a friend was waiting to drive me to the airport. I told him I had things to do in London, but I also had a book to finish and I could do that in Chicago as well, I supposed, as anywhere else. I would come back the following month and stay there with him while I did the work. 'That's fine,' he said. I took him up in my arms. His insubstantiality shocked me. He was like a cloud. What had I to offer him now? Already he was drifting away. 'Are you afraid of anything?' I asked him. 'No,' he said. His eyes were wide and looking out beyond me somewhere.

I went back to London. Letty called me a week later to tell me that my father had been engulfed in an entirely sleepless 48-hour-long hallucination during which he barely stopped moving. She barricaded one of the exits from his room with a heap of furniture but he dismantled it. When I had been there he barely had the strength to stand. He lay down for a little while, but then in the middle of the night she found him roaming again.

'What are you looking for?' she asked him.

'For my chequebook,' he said.

'What for?'

'There's a man waiting in the living room and I have to pay him.'

'What do you have to pay him for?'

'For my funeral services,' he said.

When it was over he slept for fifteen hours and when he woke he was himself again. I called him.

'What was that about?' I asked him.

'I don't know,' he said. 'But it's left me very tired.'

The book I was writing was a novel containing

161

pictures by the photographer Steve Pyke. Three days after that conversation with my father, Steve and I travelled to Ireland together to get the last of the pictures. It was 15 October. I was by then long apart from Teresa and our daughter Aoife. I was on my own. When we flew to Dublin no one knew where we were going. We didn't know ourselves. After we landed we went around the bars. We met a couple of friends in Wynne's Hotel and then walked over to the Flowing Tide, across the street from the Abbey Theatre. Just after closing time a cousin of Teresa's whom I hadn't seen in many years walked through the dim light to our table. She told me her husband had a message for me. What I didn't know was that calls had gone from Letty to my home in London and to several other numbers, including Teresa's, and that Teresa had phoned everyone she knew in Dublin to ask if they'd seen me. Her cousin had been found at the Abbey Theatre, and out of all the bars in Dublin had walked into the one I was in. I went with her to a phone and called her husband. It was from him that I learned my father had died. He'd stood up beside his bed at noon and then sat down again. He told Letty that he couldn't make it. He lay down on the bed then and the life went out of him.

I went back to Chicago and moved around the rooms filled with the furniture of my childhood. It had the feeling of the stillborn about it.

Everything was dusted and put away and the bed on which he'd died was neatly made. Bottles of his medicine were on a little tray in the kitchen. I tried to pick up some sense of him in the air but I couldn't. It was vacant. He'd stood on his feet for fifty-five years looking into people's mouths. He'd won a charleston contest. He had drunk in speakeasies and on the streets of Havana and when he was small he felled a local bully with a lucky punch. He had a gift for telling stories. He'd shot sub-par golf. He'd found a woman who had never ceased to fascinate him. He was kind and steady and severe and glamorous. He was the one truly heroic figure of my life. He'd arrived at the point where everything was fading and dimming and where his mind was tethered to his decrepitude. Now he was free.

At the funeral I looked at the coppery sheen on his coffin and realized that all the things that kept occurring to me to tell him would remain for ever unspoken. I had the idea of getting in his car and living for a while in motels by the side of the road as I headed south, maybe all the way down through Mexico to Guatemala. I could write the rest of my book that way maybe. But I didn't do it. I stayed in Chicago and cleared away his things – his furniture and pictures and books, his trousers and shoes and hats. I found a leather box with a loose hinge containing pens and nail files and combs, fine strands of his silver hair still caught between the teeth. There was a letter he'd written to his father from the Pacific when he was with the Navy during the war. There was a photograph of my mother laughing as she faced a wild bear in a forest in North Carolina. There were key rings, holy medals and golf scorecards. There was a little printed homily about golf written by someone named David R. Forgan with 'From E. J. O'Grady' typed at the bottom, and there was the note Arnold Palmer had written to him when I'd played with him at Bay Hill – 'To Ed, Sorry you couldn't be here for the golf. Tim was good. Best wishes, Arnold Palmer.' There was a poem about fathers and sons which he'd cut from a newspaper, the paper yellow and the edges jagged where his hands had been unsteady, and which I could not read to the end the first or the second or even the fifth time I attempted it.

I'd never asked him what he would have said had he been at the Scottish dinner in Michael Murphy's book. Perhaps if I had I wouldn't have got an answer, but I think it likelier that he would have tried. Whatever golf is – an escape from quotidian life, a lark, a livelihood, a lifelong dialogue – to speak about it is only a game and I am sure he would have participated because he enjoyed games and they made him laugh. What would he have said? I cannot know. I have only that small printed page with his name typed at the bottom which I found in his leather box. As I sifted through his things I found several more of them in desk drawers, envelopes and stuck in among the pages of books. Where had they all come from? It read,

Golf – An Appreciation

It is a science – the study of a lifetime, in which you may exhaust yourself but never your subject. It is a contest, a duel or melee, calling for courage, skill, strategy and self-control. It is a test of temper, a trial of honor, a revealer of character. It affords the chance to play the man and act the gentleman. It means going into God's out-of-doors, getting close to nature, fresh air, exercise, a sweeping away of mental cobwebs, general recreation of the tired tissues. It is a cure for care – an antidote to worry. It includes companionship with friends, social intercourse, opportunity for courtesy, kindliness and generosity to an opponent. It promotes not only physical health but moral force.

This was him on the golf course, I thought, or at least a part of him – though he would have expressed it more simply and directly. He learned and he taught, he searched for ideas, he was genial in company, he sought the catharsis of the hard-hit shot in the open air. He was fair, honest, gracious. I knew about his moral force because he'd wasted me with it when I'd lied or been deficient in respect. He was drawn both to the solitary trial of self and the chance to compete and win. I think he liked the idea of facing up to the exposure all this entailed. If golf reveals character, as the piece says, then I would say he was vindicated through his relationship to it.

He was better than me in all of this and in the level of his play. If golf reveals character then I find mine stained here and there with petulance, victimhood, envy and schadenfreude. Also vanity, through the pursuit of the glorious shot instead of the kind of play that wins matches. I can still learn from him in these things. I think of the way he was with a golf club, how balanced and sure and intimate, how taut with concentration, the head down, the hands moving forward and out. I think of him going at it one-handed when he cracked a rib, of the three wood he rifled at the man who had bombarded my mother and me, of that last low line drive he hit to the edge of the green when he was eighty-six. I look for him, for the soundness of his ball-striking, his dignity while enduring bad play, his tenacity and focus, and in the controlled and sure act of faith and release that was his golf swing.

I would like to thank Steve Carr for his help on many occasions in acquiring information and for reading the manuscript. Geoff Mulligan, at the time working at *Esquire*, was the first to ask me to write about golf. Robert Green, Rosie Boycott and Melanie Garrett, as well as Steve Carr, sent me to interview great players and to play on wonderful courses. The late Harry Campbell supplied me with an important book and was the Scot I had in mind when writing p. 4. Nick Groom sent me Thomas Mathison's poem mentioned on p. 75. Doc Giffen arranged the round with Arnold Palmer. The joke about the petulant American and his Scots caddy on p. 30 appeared in James Dodson's book *Final Rounds*. The journalist who conducted the interview with Earl Woods mentioned on p. 84 is Lawrence Donegan. I had long wished to write a book about golf without knowing what it might be, until Dan Franklin told me about the series of which this book is a part. Rachel Cugnoni then invited me to write it and has stayed close to it since. Tristan Jones edited it with acute sensitivity.

The author and publishers would like to make grateful acknowledgement to the following for permission to reproduce previously published material: 'The Back Nine' by Loudon Wainwright III Copyright © 1986 Snowden Music, Inc. All rights reserved. Used by permission; Russell & Volkening Literary Agency, New York, for *The Bogey Man* by George Plimpton (HarperCollins); Penguin Group (UK) for *Rabbit, Run* by John Updike (Penguin) and *Golf Dreams* by John Updike (Hamish Hamilton); Random House Group Ltd for *Beyond a Boundary* by C. L. R. James (Hutchinson) and 'Rodney Fails to Qualify', from *The Heart of a Goof* by P. G. Wodehouse (Hutchinson); David Higham Associates for *The Great Gatsby* by F. Scott Fitzgerald (Penguin); John Murray for 'Seaside Golf', from *Collected Poems* by John Betjeman (John Murray); Mainstream Publishing for *To the Linksland* by Michael Bamburger (Mainstream); and Penguin Group (USA) for 'Singing the Praises of Golf', from *Golf in the Kingdom* by Michael Murphy (Viking Penguin).

The photograph on p. ii is of the author aged two. The photograph on p. 167 is of his father, Edward J. O'Grady.